BEST OF
Aleene's Creative Living®
Book 3

Oxmoor House®

Best of Aleene's Creative Living, Book 3
©1999 by Oxmoor House, Inc.
Book Division of Southern Progress Corporation
P.O. Box 2463, Birmingham, Alabama 35201

Published by Oxmoor House, Inc., and Leisure Arts, Inc.

Library of Congress Catalog Card Number: 97-65762
Hardcover ISBN: 0-8487-1911-5
Softcover ISBN: 0-8487-1912-3
Printed in the United States of America
First Printing 1999

Editor-in-Chief: Nancy Fitzpatrick Wyatt
Senior Crafts Editor: Susan Ramey Cleveland
Senior Editor, Copy and Homes: Olivia Kindig Wells
Art Director: James Boone

Best of Aleene's Creative Living, Book 3
Editor: Lois Martin
Editorial Assistant: Heather Averett
Copy Editor: L. Amanda Owens
Contributing Designer: Carol Damsky
Illustrator: Kelly Davis
Director, Production and Distribution: Phillip Lee
Associate Production Managers: James McDaniel, Vanessa Richardson
Production Assistant: Faye Porter Bonner

Aleene's Creative Living
Founder: Aleene Jackson
Editor: Tiffany M. Windsor
Managing Editor: Cathy J. Burlingham
Assistant Editor: Joan Fee
Director of Photography: Craig Cook
Senior Photographer: Medeighnia Lentz
Designer/Stylist: Carolyn Bainbridge
Cover Portrait Photographer: Christine Photography

To order Aleene's products by mail, call Aleene's in California at 1-800-825-3363.

Projects pictured on front cover (clockwise from top left): Golden Angels, page 136; Holly Necklace, page 84; Silver & Gold, page 74; and Floral Hearts, page 32. Project pictured on back cover: Garden Party, page 20.

We're Here for You!
We at Oxmoor House are dedicated to serving you with reliable information that expands your imagination and enriches your life. We welcome your comments and suggestions. Please write us at:
Oxmoor House, Inc.
Editor, *Best of Aleene's Creative Living, Book 3*
2100 Lakeshore Drive
Birmingham, AL 35209
To order additional publications, call 1-205-877-6560.

Aleene   Heidi

Introduction

Best of Aleene's Creative Living, Book 3 offers you some of our favorite craft projects for home decor, wearables, gifts, and holiday decorations.

These projects have made it through two selection rounds. Every month, the editorial staff of *Aleene's Creative Living* magazine reviews more than 200 craft projects presented in a month of television shows and selects about 40 of these to include in the magazine. We look for projects that represent a variety of craft types, skill levels, and uses. Thanks to the support of national crafts stores and major manufacturers, plus the work of top independent designers, we're able to present our readers with fresh, new crafts that feature innovative products and brand-new techniques.

Then the magazine staff teams up with the staff of Oxmoor House to review projects that have been published in the magazine and to choose a collection of outstanding crafts. We've previously published two volumes of *Best of Aleene's Creative Living*. Now, we gladly offer more superb projects in *Best of Aleene's Creative Living, Book 3*. We hope you enjoy making these projects.

Wishing you endless creativity,

Heidi

3

Contents

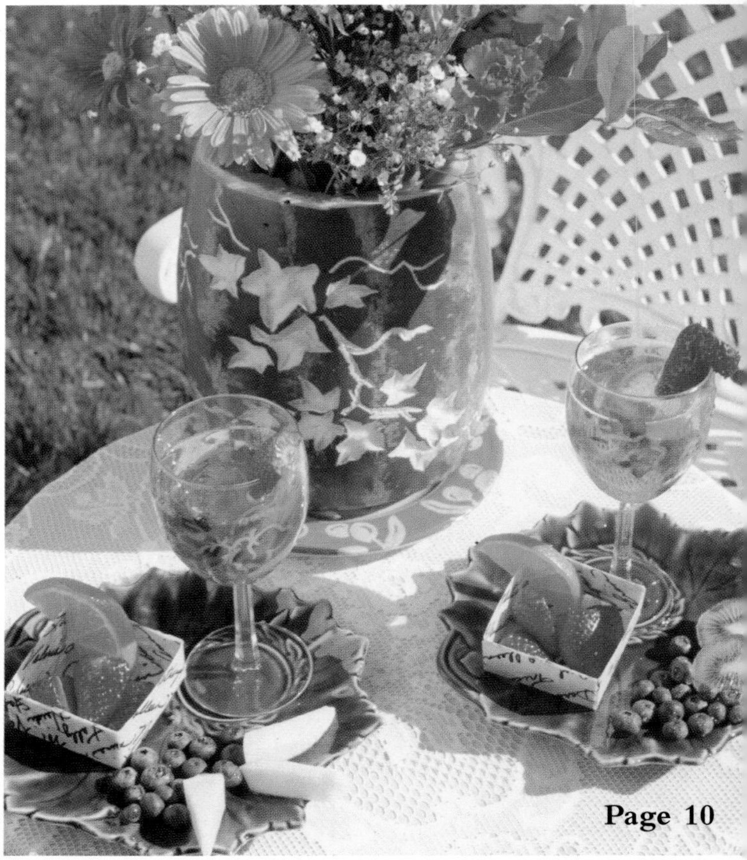

Page 10

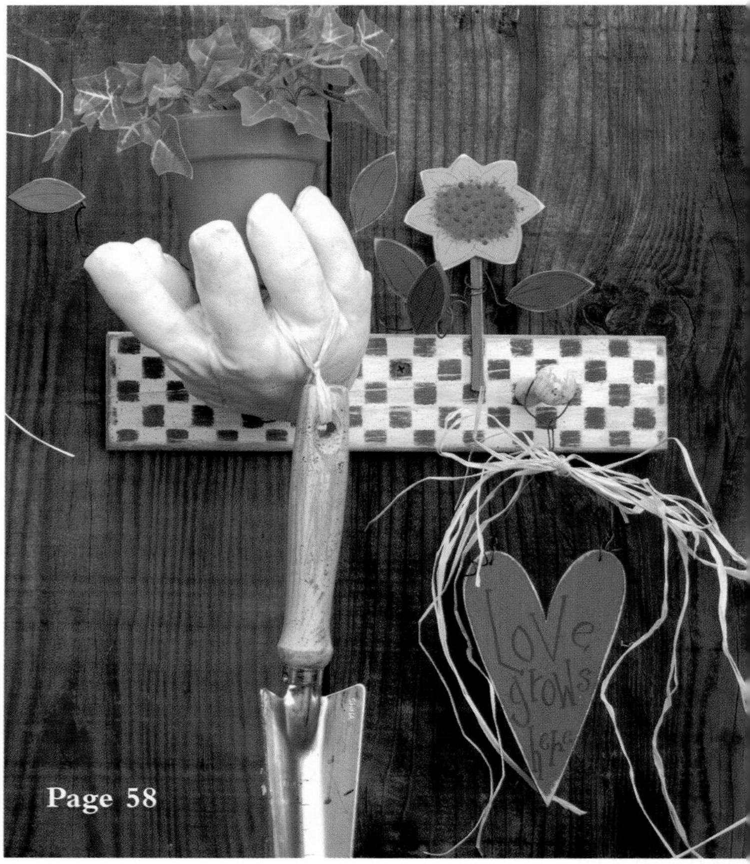

Page 58

Page 82

Page 120

GIVE THANKS

Crafting Hints

Each project includes a materials list. In addition to these specific items, your craft room should be stocked with a few basic items. You may need to look elsewhere in your home for common household items and appliances that do not appear on individual project materials lists.

Before beginning any craft project, have on hand two pairs of sharp scissors: one for cutting paper and the other for cutting fabric. (Cutting paper dulls scissors faster than cutting fabric, so extend the life of fabric scissors by reserving them exclusively for that purpose.)

To complete many of the projects in the book, you need paper towels and water in a container. A sharp, soft-lead (#2) pencil and scrap paper are also handy additions to your craft room.

To work with fusible web (see right), you need an iron and ironing board or other flat surface. To work with Shrink-It™ plastic, you need a toaster or a conventional oven. You can speed the drying process for some types of paint and glue by using a handheld hairdryer.

Tips for Successful Gluing

Aleene and Heidi give you the benefit of their years of crafting experience with the following suggestions for working with glue.

• To make Aleene's Tacky Glue™ and Aleene's Designer Tacky Glue™ even tackier, leave the lid off for about an hour before use so that excess moisture evaporates.

• Too much glue makes items slip around; it does not provide a better bond. To apply a film of glue to a project, use a cardboard squeegee (see photo below). Cut a 3" square of cardboard (cereal box cardboard works well) and use this squeegee to smooth the glue onto the craft material. Wait a few minutes to let the glue begin to form a skin before putting the items together.

Use a cardboard squeegee to apply glue.

• To squeeze fine lines of glue from a glue bottle, apply a temporary tape tip to the bottle nozzle. Using a 4"-long piece of transparent tape, align 1 long edge of the tape with the nozzle edge. Press the tape firmly to the nozzle to prevent leaks. Rotate the glue bottle to wrap the tape around the nozzle. The tape will reverse direction and wind back down toward the bottle. Press the tail of the tape to the bottle for easy removal.

Working with Aleene's Fusible Web™

Wash and dry fabrics and garments to remove any sizing before applying fusible web. Do not use fabric softener in the washer or the dryer. Transfer the pattern to the paper side of the web and cut out the pattern as specified in the project directions.

Lay the fabric wrong side up on an ironing surface. A hard surface, such as a wooden cutting board, ensures a firm bond. Lay the fusible web, paper side up, on the fabric (the glue side feels rough). With a hot, dry iron, fuse web to fabric by placing and lifting the iron. Do not allow the iron to rest on the web for more than 2 or 3 seconds. Do not slide the iron back and forth across the web.

To fuse the cutout to the project, carefully peel the paper backing from the cutout, making sure the web is attached to the fabric (see photo, page 7). If the web is still attached to the paper, fuse it again to the fabric cutout before fusing it to the

Transfer patterns to the paper side of fusible web and then fuse them to the wrong side of fabric.

Metric Conversion Chart

U.S.	Metric
⅛"	3 mm
¼"	6 mm
⅜"	9 mm
½"	1.3 cm
⅝"	1.6 cm
¾"	1.9 cm
⅞"	2.2 cm
1"	2.5 cm
2"	5.1 cm
3"	7.6 cm
4"	10.2 cm
5"	12.7 cm
6"	15.2 cm
7"	17.8 cm
8"	20.3 cm
9"	22.9 cm
10"	25.4 cm
11"	27.9 cm
12"	30.5 cm
36"	91.5 cm
45"	114.3 cm
60"	152.4 cm
⅛ yard	0.11 m
¼ yard	0.23 m
⅓ yard	0.3 m
⅜ yard	0.34 m
½ yard	0.46 m
⅝ yard	0.57 m
⅔ yard	0.61 m
¾ yard	0.69 m
⅞ yard	0.8 m
1 yard	0.91 m

To Convert to Metric Measurements:

When you know:	Multiply by:	To find:
inches (")	25	millimeters (mm)
inches (")	2.5	centimeters (cm)
inches (")	0.025	meters (m)
feet (')	30	centimeters (cm)
feet (')	0.3	meters (m)
yards	90	centimeters (cm)
yards	0.9	meters (m)

project. Arrange the cutout on the project surface. With a hot, dry iron, fuse the cutout to the project by placing and lifting the iron. Hold the iron on each area of the cutout for 60 seconds.

Working with Aleene's Shrink-It™ Plastic

To work with Shrink-It, you need fine-grade sandpaper, Aleene's Baking Board or a non-stick cookie sheet, baby powder, a fine-tip black permanent marker, and colored pencils.

Sprinkle the Baking Board or the cookie sheet with baby powder. Preheat a toaster or a conventional oven to 275° to 300°.

Sand 1 side of each piece of Shrink-It so that markings will adhere. Be sure to sand thoroughly both vertically and horiztonally.

Using the black marker, trace the designs onto the sanded side of the Shrink-It. (Marker ink may run on the sanded surface, but runs will shrink and disappear during baking.) Shrink-It has a grain, so be sure to orient each design on the Shrink-It sheet the same way. This ensures that all designs will be similar in size and shape after shrinking.

Use colored pencils to color each design. Colors will be more intense after shrinking. Cut out the designs as desired from Shrink-It.

Place each design on a room-temperature baking board and bake in the preheated oven. Edges should begin to curl within 25 seconds; if not, increase temperature slightly. If edges begin to curl as soon as designs are put in oven, reduce temperature. After about 1 minute, design will lie flat. Remove each design from oven and shape according to specific project directions. Let cool.

Decorative

In the following pages, you'll find fantastic ideas for all sorts of fast and fun projects to adorn your home.

Page 30

Accents

Afternoon DELIGHT

Use stencils to turn a watermelon into an unexpected centerpiece. Create matching goblets from inexpensive glassware and then fashion coordinating fruit boxes with Aleene's BoxMaker™.

Materials

For stenciled fruit and goblets:
Aleene's Stencil Storybook™: Garden Collection

For stenciled fruit: Watermelon
Large kitchen knife
Curved kitchen knife or fruit scoop
Lemon juice
Clear plastic wrap
Vase or votive cup to fit inside fruit
Fresh flowers or votive candle

For 1 stenciled goblet: 1 glass goblet
Acrylic paints for glass: green, purple
Sponge brush
Cotton swabs
Gold paint pen

For 1 waxed fruit box: Fine-tip permanent black marker
Aleene's BoxBlanks™
Aleene's BoxMaker™
Aleene's Ultimate Glue Gun™
Aleene's All-Purpose Glue Sticks™
Candle wax or paraffin
Tongs
Waxed paper
Fruit, chocolate candies, or other treats to fill box

Directions for stenciled fruit

1 On protected work surface, cut off rounded end of watermelon to create flat bottom, using large kitchen knife. Stand watermelon on flat end and cut off top. Scoop out fruit and save for another use.

2 Tape stencil to surface of watermelon where desired. Trace design with point of large knife. Remove stencil. Carve out shallow design to allow inside color of rind to show, using curved knife or fruit scoop (see photo). Moisten stenciled area with lemon juice. Cover with plastic wrap until ready to display.

3 To use, remove plastic wrap and place vase of fresh flowers or votive cup with candle into finished fruit.

Directions for stenciled goblet

Cut stencil design apart as desired. Tape desired portion of stencil onto goblet (see photo). Sponge-paint design with desired paint colors. Carefully remove

Designs by Pattie Donham

stencil. Wipe off any smudges with cotton swabs. Let dry. Draw leaf veins or trace edge of leaves as desired, using paint pen.

Directions for waxed fruit box

1 Use permanent marker to write names or phrases on both sides of BoxBlanks.

2 Cut 5½" square from BoxBlanks. Use BoxMaker to score square at 1½" line. Following manufacturer's instructions, cut notches in corners of square. Fold along score lines. Use ribbon nozzle of glue gun to glue flaps inside box. Let dry.

3 Melt wax in pan at lowest possible temperature. (Wax should be deep enough to submerge box.) Use tongs to dip box into wax. Place box upside down onto waxed paper. Let harden. Fill box with desired treats.

Design by Cheryl Ball, SCD

An old pair of jeans becomes the perfect caddy.
No sewing required!

Materials
Old jeans
Aleene's OK To Wash-It Glue™
Masking tape
Aluminum foil
Belt

1 Cut off back pockets, taking care not to pull out stitching. Set pockets aside. Lay jeans faceup on work surface. Align inside leg seams with zipper. Tuck excess fabric below zipper to create smooth line (see photo). Following inseams, glue legs together from crotch to hem. Hold in place with masking tape while drying; then remove tape.

2 Lift front waistband and apply liberal amount of glue to back inside seam of jeans. Press front of jeans into glue along zipper to form 2 large pockets. Let dry.

3 Fold jeans about 4" below zipper so that waistband meets knee area (see photo). Glue back waistband to legs of jeans, leaving side belt loops open. Let dry.

4 Place aluminum foil in each front pocket to keep glue from seeping through. Apply glue to 3 edges of set–aside back pockets and press each to front of keeper (see photo). Let dry. Remove aluminum foil. Run belt under glued waistband and through belt loops (see photo); buckle belt.

5 To use, place pant legs between mattress and box spring (see photo).

Earth Angel

A little paint and glue transform common clay pots into a charming ornament for your porch or patio.

Materials

Aleene's Premium-Coat™ Acrylic
    Paints: Black, Medium Fuchsia,
    White
Liner paintbrush
2½" wooden apple
Clay pots: 4 (1½"-diameter),
    4 (2½"-diameter),
    1 (3"-diameter)
Aleene's Ultimate Glue Gun™
Aleene's All-Purpose Glue Sticks™
Aleene's Thick Designer Tacky Glue
Green, Spanish moss
Birch branches
Florist's wire
Wire cutters
2 (3"-diameter) grapevine wreaths
Raffia scrap
3 sunflower buttons
3 artificial sunflowers

Directions

1 Using Black and liner brush, paint ⅜"-diameter circles on wooden apple for eyes; then paint mouth (see photo). Let dry. For cheeks, paint ½"-diameter Medium Fuchsia circles. Highlight eyes with white paint. Let dry.

2 For legs, turn 2 (2½") clay pots upside down and glue sheet moss to bottom and sides of each (see photo). Use glue gun for instant hold; then use Tacky Glue for permanent hold. Let dry. Stack 1 (2½") pot on top of each and glue in place. Let dry. For arms, turn 2 (1½") clay pots upside down and glue sheet moss to bottom and sides of each (see photo). Let dry. Stack 1 (1½") pot on top of each and glue in place. Let dry.

3 Glue sheet moss inside rim of (3") clay pot. Turn (3") pot upside down. Let dry. Referring to photo, glue legs to rim and arms to sides of (3") pot. Let dry. Glue sheet moss across neck and shoulder area. Glue wooden apple in place for head and Spanish moss in place for hair. Let dry.

4 For wings, cut birch branches into 8" to 10" pieces. Wire together in center, using florist's wire. Glue wings to back of angel (see photo). Let dry. For halo, cut 3" piece of birch branch and glue to back of head. Glue 1 grapevine wreath to top of branch. Let dry.

5 Tie raffia bow and glue at neck. Let dry. Glue 1 sunflower button in center of raffia bow. Glue remaining buttons down center front of body. Let dry. Cut remaining grapevine wreath apart. Extend between arms and glue inside arm pots to secure (see photo). Let dry. Glue sunflowers beside 1 arm.

Recycle an old frame or other found object into a useful jewelry organizer with some screen and a little ingenuity.

Materials for each organizer

Aleene's Premium-Coat™ Acrylic Paints: Black, Gold (optional)
Paintbrush
Frame (or other item with open area for mesh)
Mesh screening (available at hardware stores)
Staple gun and staples
Florist's wire (optional)
Wire cutters (optional)
Black spray paint (optional)
Kitchen sponge (optional)
Aleene's Right-On™ Finish

Directions

Paint frame Black. Let dry. Cut mesh screening 1" larger than frame opening, using old scissors. Staple screening to back of frame. (If using other item, you may need to use florist's wire to attach screening to object.) If desired, spray-paint mesh black. Let dry. For antiqued look, sponge-paint frame with Gold. (see photo). Let dry. Apply 1 coat of Right-On Finish. Let dry.

Designs by Darsee Lett and Pattie Donham

SCREEN SAVERS

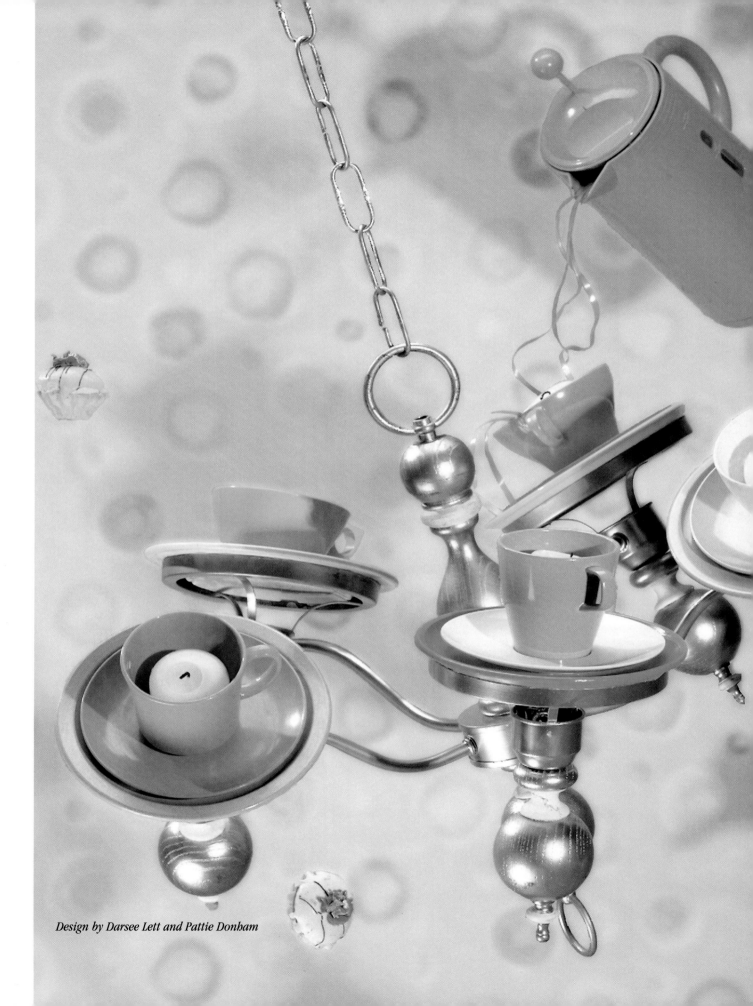

Design by Darsee Lett and Pattie Donham

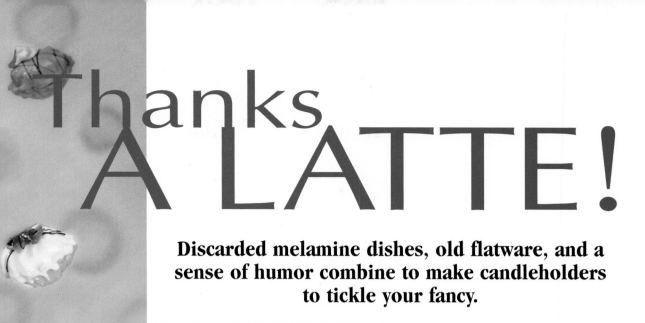

Thanks
A LATTE!

Discarded melamine dishes, old flatware, and a sense of humor combine to make candleholders to tickle your fancy.

Materials

For each: **Spray paint in desired colors**
Aleene's Ultimate Glue Gun™
Aleene's All-Purpose Glue Sticks™
For chandelier: **Old chandelier**
Assorted melamine plates, saucers, and cups
E-6000® Glue (optional)
Minipillar candles
For 1 candleholder: **Melamine cup and saucer**
Electric drill with S/32 metal bit
3 thin metal spoons
3 nuts and 3 bolts (to fit size of bit)
Candle to fit cup

Directions for chandelier

1. Remove electrical wires and fixtures from chandelier. Spray-paint chandelier and chain in desired color. Let dry. If desired, spray-paint melamine dishes in desired colors. Let dry.

2. Put small amount of E-6000 or hot glue on bottom of 1 plate and secure to 1 arm of chandelier. Let dry. Repeat to glue saucer to plate. Let dry. Then glue cup to saucer. Let dry. Repeat to glue 1 plate-saucer-cup set to each remaining arm of chandelier. Let dry.

3. Place 1 candle in each cup. Hang chandelier from chain.

Directions for candleholder

1. If desired, spray-paint cup and saucer in desired colors. Let dry.

2. Drill 3 holes near center of saucer. Drill 1 hole 1" from end of each spoon handle. Match hole in 1 spoon with 1 hole in saucer; push 1 bolt through hole and secure with 1 nut. Repeat to attach 2 more spoons to saucer. Bend spoons to make feet for candle stand (see photo below).

3. Put hot glue on bottom of cup and place on saucer. Let dry. Set candle inside cup.

TIP: For another whimsical touch with old cups and saucers, stack and glue 2 or more sets together and place candle inside top cup.

Garden Party

Stiffen a circle of muslin to fit an inexpensive side table and then sponge-paint it with a garden design. Go on to make a matching teapot—and your party is ready to begin.

Materials
For each: Pop-up craft sponges
Aleene's Premium-Coat™ Acrylic Paints in desired colors
⅛"-wide paintbrush
For table: Wooden side table
Muslin (yardage equals table diameter plus 12")
Cardboard covered with waxed paper (should be larger than muslin)
Aleene's Fabric Stiffener™
3" cardboard squeegee
String (enough to go around edge of table and tie)
Paper towels
For teapot: Mâché Teapot by D&CC
Aleene's Premium-Coat™ Acrylic Paint: Ivory
1"-wide sponge paintbrush

Directions for table

1 From muslin, cut circle 12" larger than table diameter. Place muslin circle on cardboard covered with waxed paper. Pour fabric stiffener onto muslin and squeegee over surface of muslin. Remove excess stiffener. Repeat on remaining side of muslin.

2 Place muslin on top of side table. Smooth out any wrinkles and make sure edges are even (see photo). Tie string around edge of table top to hold muslin flat against table. Let dry. Then remove string.

3 Transfer patterns to sponges and cut out. Place each sponge into water to expand and squeeze out excess water. Dip each sponge into desired color paint; blot excess paint on paper towel. Press sponge onto table top where desired (see photo for inspiration). Wash sponge thoroughly before dipping into different color paint. Let dry.

4 Paint around edges of flowers freehand, using brush and coordinating paint colors (see photo). Paint centers of flowers as desired. Let dry.

5 Paint wavy lines around edge of table and edge of muslin skirt and then paint stripes swirling up table legs, using desired colors (see photo). Let dry.

Directions for teapot

Using Ivory and sponge brush, paint teapot. Let dry. Referring to photo, follow steps 3 and 4 for table to sponge-paint teapot designs. Let dry. Using ⅛" paintbrush, add vines to spout and handle as desired.

21

Starswirls!

Stamp your way to a masterpiece. It's so easy, a child can do it.

Materials for each frame
9"-square frame
Aleene's Premium-Coat™ Acrylic
   Paints in desired colors
Paintbrushes
Low-tack masking tape
Foam stamps: star, swirl
Plastic-coated paper plate
Pencil with eraser (optional)

Directions

Note: Before working with frame, practice stamping images on scrap paper to choose colors and placement.

1 Paint frame desired color. Let dry. To create stripes, squares, or other geometric shapes (see photos), cover desired areas of painted frame with masking tape; paint second color on untaped areas. Let dry. Then remove tape.

2 To stamp designs, pour small amount of desired color paint onto paper plate. Apply paint to desired foam stamp, using brush. Stamp frame as desired, applying even pressure to stamp. (Do not rock or wiggle.) Carefully lift stamp

directly off frame. Blot stamp on scrap paper to remove excess paint before reapplying paint or changing paint colors. (Reapply paint before making each impression to get uniform images.) Let dry.

3 To paint thin lines, use small paintbrush. To paint dots, dip end of paintbrush or pencil eraser into paint and dot on frame as desired. Let dry.

Designs by Grace Taormina

Just Like NEW!

Shop garage sales and thrift stores for inexpensive trays to turn into festive accessories.

Materials for each tray
Serving tray
Fine-grit sandpaper
Tack cloth
Black spray paint
Aleene's Decoupage Papers™ in desired design
Aleene's Instant Decoupage™
2 foam paintbrushes
Aleene's Premium-Coat™ Acrylic Paints in desired colors
Paint pens in desired colors

Directions

1 Lightly sand tray. Wipe with tack cloth to remove dust. Spray-paint entire tray black. Let dry.

2 Cut out desired portion of decoupage paper to decorate inside flat area of tray (see photo). Apply Instant Decoupage to underside of cutout, using 1 foam paintbrush. Position on tray as desired, pressing out wrinkles and bubbles, using fingers. Apply 1 coat of Instant Decoupage over entire surface of tray. Let dry.

3 Paint squares and shading in desired colors of acrylic paint, using remaining foam paintbrush (see photo). Let dry. Use paint pens to highlight edges of flowers and to add dots and other details as desired. Let dry. Then write sayings, poems, or desired words on tray, using paint pens. Let dry.

Designs by Pattie Donham

Natural Lighting

Place these easy-to-make accent lights on an indoor table or use them outdoors in good weather.

Materials for each lamp
Wire tomato cage
Foam-core board (at least diameter of tomato cage plus ¼")
Craft knife (optional)
Parchment paper
Aleene's Thick Designer Tacky Glue™
Aleene's Ultimate Glue Gun™
Aleene's All-Purpose Glue Sticks™
1 strand Christmas lights (low-wattage minilights only)
Florist's wire
Wire cutters
Ice pick
Curly willow or birch twigs

Directions

Note: Handle finished project carefully due to fragile nature of paper. Do not leave unattended when lights are plugged in.

1 For base, set tomato cage on foam-core board. Trace ¼" around outside edge of cage. Cut out foam-core board, using scissors or craft knife. Cover entire board with parchment paper, using Tacky Glue. Let dry.

2 Spread out remaining parchment paper. Place cage on its side in center of paper. Squeeze hot glue along 1 long wire, from top to bottom of cage. Repeat along next long wire and roll cage to glue paper to wires. Let dry. Trim paper along second glued wire. Squeeze hot glue along second long wire again (on top of paper) and onto next long wire; roll cage to glue paper to wires. Let dry. Trim paper. Repeat gluing and trimming process to cover entire cage. Then trim paper at top and bottom, leaving 1" beyond cage. At bottom of cage, turn paper under and glue in place to form hem. Leave paper extension at top of cage.

3 Fold lights into strands equal to length of cage. Cut 12" length of florist's wire. Wire lights together at end without plug. Insert lights into cage, pushing wire out of top. Wind wire around top of cage to secure lights.

4 Set lighted cage onto foam-core base, with light cord coming out from under cage. Using ice pick, punch hole in foam-core base where each vertical wire of cage meets base. Gently punch 1 hole in paper at bottom of cage on each side of each vertical wire. Cut 12" length of wire. Thread end of wire through 1 hole in base and attach base to project at vertical wire. Repeat to attach base at remaining holes. (To change or replace lights, simply untwist wires to remove paper-covered cage from base.)

5 Attach twigs to top and bottom of cage, using florist's wire (see photo). Weave twigs around wires.

Design by Darsee Lett and Pattie Donham

Pillow Press

Use Satin Sheen™ to shape your own stamp for a unique pillow.

Materials
Purchased pillow cover
Aleene's Satin Sheen™ in any color
Aleene's Ultimate Hot Glue Gun™
Aleene's All-Purpose Glue Sticks™
4" square foam-core board
Aleene's Enhancers™ Textile Medium
Aleene's Premium-Coat™ Acrylic Paint in desired color
Disposable Brush Sticks™
Paper towels
Pillow form

Directions

1 Wash and dry pillow cover; do not use fabric softener in washer or drier. Iron as needed to remove wrinkles.

2 To make stamp, cut 12" length of Satin Sheen; do not unfold. Hot-glue Satin Sheen to foam-core board in coil design (see photo).

3 Mix equal parts textile medium and paint. Apply paint to Satin Sheen stamp, using disposable brush. Press painted stamp onto pillow cover where desired, applying even pressure. (Do not rock or wiggle.) To create clean, solid impressions, blot stamp on paper towel and repeat paint application to stamp before each use. Continue stamping until you achieve desired effect. Let dry.

4 Insert pillow form into pillow cover.

Design by Pattie Donham

A Dog's Life

Give your favorite dog (or cat) a stenciled bowl for treats or food.

Materials
Rubbing alcohol
Paper towel
Ovenproof ceramic or glass bowl
Masking tape
Aleene's Stencil Storybooks™ in desired design
Pebeo Paints in desired colors
Pebeo Gloss Medium (optional)
Paper plate
Stencil brush

Directions

1 Pour rubbing alcohol onto paper towel and clean surface of bowl. Let dry.

2 Use tape to mask off any areas of stencil you don't want to paint with first color. Attach stencil to bowl where desired, using tape. Pour small puddle of each desired paint color onto paper plate. For translucent look, add gloss medium to paint, following manufacturer's directions.

3 Dab stencil brush into desired paint and press onto stencil. Let dry. For darker colors, apply paint again; let dry. Remove tape. Tape off sections for next color.

Repeat steps 2 and 3 until all open areas of stencil are painted. Let dry 24 hours.

4 Place bowl in cold oven. Heat oven to 300° and bake for 20 minutes. Leave bowl in oven until temperature has cooled.

Design by Joan Fee

Design by Melody Ramsey

Gardener's Wreath

Ivy and miniature flowerpots become a welcoming wreath for your home.

Materials
Green felt
18"-diameter foam wreath
Aleene's Ultimate Glue Gun™
Aleene's All-Purpose Glue Sticks™
Clay pots: 12 (1"), 11 (1½"),
   6 (2"), 3 (3")
Desired wire-edged ribbon
Sheet moss
Artificial English ivy
Florist's pins
Resin pot hangers in assorted
   animal shapes

Directions

1 Cut felt to cover wreath back. Glue in place. Let dry.

2 Glue 2" and 3" pots randomly around front of wreath (see photo at left). Let dry. Cut 50" length of ribbon; tie multiloop bow with streamers. Glue bow to wreath (see photo at left). Let dry. Glue 1" and 1½" pots randomly around front of wreath. Let dry. Glue moss to cover exposed areas of wreath. Let dry.

3 Wind ivy around pots throughout wreath. Hold ivy in place with florist's pins and glue to secure. Let dry. Glue animal-shaped pot hangers to edges of pots as desired (see photos at left and right). Let dry.

Floral Hearts

Fold and sew wire-edged ribbon into assorted flowers and then stitch them to heart-shaped felt pillows.

Materials

For each: Regular sewing thread in colors to match ribbons

Needles: hand-sewing, size 20 chenille

1 skein green #5 pearl cotton

Fiberfill

For 1 small pillow: ¼ yard white felt

¼ yard each ⅞"-wide wire-edged ombre ribbons in 3 coordinating colors

1 package each 4-mm silk embroidery ribbon: gold, burgundy, green

For 1 medium pillow: ¼ yard white felt

Wire-edged ombre ribbons: ⅜ yard each 1½"-wide in 3 coordinating colors; 1 yard ⅞"-wide green

1 package each 4-mm silk embroidery ribbon: gold, green

For 1 large pillow: ⅜ yard white felt

Wire-edged ombre ribbons: ⅜ yard each 1½"-wide in 3 coordinating colors; 1 yard ⅞"-wide green

1 package each 4-mm silk embroidery ribbon: white, gold

Directions

1 **For small pillow,** cut 2 pieces of felt in heart shape, each approximately 6" x 7".

Make 1 pansy from each color of ⅞"-wide ribbon. For each flower, cut 7½" length of ribbon. Fold each end down 2¼" (see Pansy Diagram on page 34). Using hand-sewing needle and thread, make running stitches ⅛" from upper edge and across each end, leaving long tail. Pull thread to gather tightly. Sew raw edges together. Using gold or burgundy silk ribbon, make long, straight stitches in flower center (see photo).

Make 1 bud from each color of ribbon. For each bud, cut 1¾" length of ribbon and fold in half. Make running stitches across bottom of bud and pull to gather. Sew raw edges together. Arrange pansies and buds on pillow front. Tack in place.

2 **For medium pillow,** cut 2 pieces of felt in heart shape, each approximately 9" x 11".

Make 1 dahlia from each color of 1½"-wide ribbon. For each flower, cut 1 (13") length of ribbon. Make running stitches in zigzag along length of ribbon,

Designs by Ellie Schneider

using matching thread (see Dahlia Diagram) and leaving long tail. Pull thread to gather tightly. Tack points and centers in place.

Make 3 dahlia buds. For each bud, cut 3" length of ribbon, stitch zigzag as for dahlia, pull to gather, and sew raw edges together. Arrange dahlias and buds on pillow front (see photo on pages 32 and 33). Tack in place. Make 4 or 5 French knots in center of each dahlia, using gold silk ribbon.

3 **For large pillow,** cut 2 heart-shaped pieces of felt, each approximately 11" x 13".

Make 1 pansy from each color of 1½"-wide ribbon, following directions for small pillow. Make 3 buds, using 3½" lengths of ribbon. Arrange pansies and buds on pillow front (see photo). Tack in place. Make 4 or 5 straight stitches in center of each pansy, using white silk ribbon.

4 **For each,** make 3 flower stems by twisting green ribbon tightly between fingers (see Twisted Stem Diagram). Use 11" lengths of green silk ribbon for small pillow, 12" lengths of green ombre ribbon for medium

pillow, or 13" lengths of green ombre ribbon for large pillow. Position each stem on pillow (see photo) and tack in place, tucking stem under flowers and spreading ribbon over buds. Take long straight stitches across lower edge of each bud to cover raw edges. Secure ends with glue or handstitches.

5 To finish pillow, blanket-stitch front to back, with wrong sides together and raw edges aligned, using pearl cotton (see Blanket-stitch Diagram) and leaving opening for stuffing. Stuff pillow, using fiberfill. Blanket-stitch opening closed.

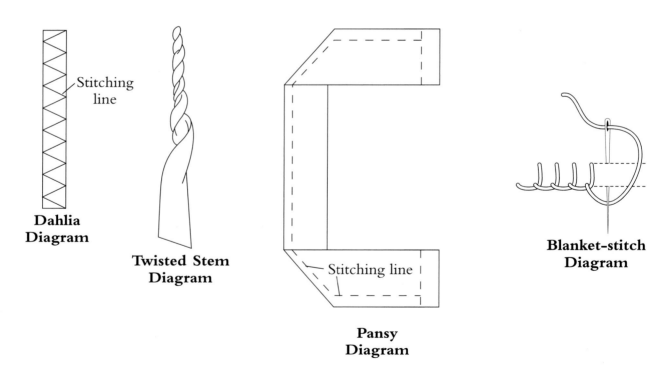

Dahlia Diagram

Stitching line

Twisted Stem Diagram

Pansy Diagram

Stitching line

Blanket-stitch Diagram

Sheer Splendor

Introduce color to sheer curtains with bright tissue-paper appliqués. Or choose white tissue paper for a subtle impression. Use a real leaf as a pattern.

Materials
Sheer curtains
Aleene's Fusible Web™
Aleene's Tissue Paper™ in desired color
Desired leaf
Aleene's Paper Napkin Appliqué Glue™
Aleene's Premium Designer Brush™: #12 shader

Directions
Note: See page 6 for tips on working with fusible web.

Wash and dry curtains; do not use fabric softener in washer or dryer. Iron as needed to remove wrinkles. Fuse web to 1 side of tissue paper. Using real leaf as pattern, cut leaf shapes from fusible web-backed tissue paper. Remove paper backing from tissue cutouts. Position leaves on curtains where desired. To protect fabric, place paper backing from fusible web over tissue-paper leaves. Fuse leaves in place. To seal, brush Napkin Appliqué Glue over each tissue-paper leaf. Let dry.

Design by Cathy Burlingham

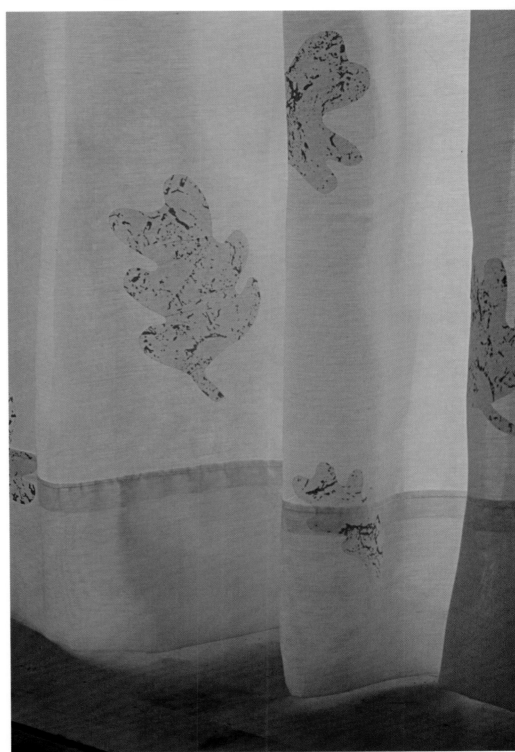

Kaleidoscope of Colors

Stencils make painting the geometric designs on these lamps fun and easy.

3-Drawer Table Lamp

Materials
Aleene's Decorator Wooden Lamps™: 3-drawer table lamp, rectangular lamp, picture-frame lamp
1 (4" x 7" x 11") Aleene's Decorator Lampshade™ for each lamp
Aleene's Enhancers™: All-Purpose Primer, Stencil Medium, Satin Varnish,
Paintbrushes: ¾" flat, sponge
Sandpaper
Tack cloth
Aleene's Premium-Coat™ Acrylic Paints: Medium Lime, Medium Turquoise, Medium Fuchsia, Medium Yellow
Drafting tape
Stencils: wavy lines, circles, zigzag, straight lines

Directions

1 **For each,** apply 1 coat of primer to lamp and shade, using flat brush. Let dry. Sand lamp lightly. Wipe lamp with tack cloth to remove dust.

2 **For 3-drawer table lamp,** paint 2"-wide horizontal stripe at top of shade, using Medium Lime. Let dry. (Use drafting tape to mark edges of each stripe; remove tape after paint dries.) Then mark and paint 2½"-wide center stripe, using Medium Turquoise. Let dry. Paint remainder of shade Medium Fuchsia. Let dry. Paint top drawer Medium Lime, center drawer Medium Turquoise, and bottom drawer Medium Fuchsia, using flat brush. Let dry. Paint sides, top, and back of lamp base Medium Fuchsia. Let dry. Paint 2 knobs Medium Turquoise and remaining knob Medium Fuchsia. Let dry. Paint top edge of base and bottom of base Medium Turquoise. Let dry.

3 For each color of paint used in stenciling, mix 2 parts acrylic paint and 1 part Stencil Medium. (Use drafting tape to protect sections of lampshade not being painted; remove tape after paint dries.) Stencil wavy line on top stripe of shade, using Medium Yellow and sponge brush. Reposition stencil as needed so that design remains vertical and repeat until pattern is complete around top stripe of shade. Let dry. Stencil wavy lines onto top drawer, using Medium Yellow. Let dry.

4 Stencil circles on center stripe of shade and and center drawer of lamp, using Medium Fuchsia. Let dry. Stencil circles on sides of lamp base, using Medium Lime on 1 side and Medium Yellow on remaining side. Then stencil circles on back of lamp base, using Medium Turquoise. Let dry.

5 Use drafting tape to cover every other row on zigzag stencil. For bottom stripe of shade and bottom drawer of lamp, stencil zigzags, using Medium Lime. Let dry.

6 Apply 1 coat of varnish to entire lamp, using flat brush. Let dry.

7 **For rectangular and picture-frame lamps,** refer to steps 1–5 and photo below for suggested colors and designs.

Designs by Bonnie Stephens

Rectangular Lamp

Picture-frame Lamp

Star Light, Star Bright

**Don't throw away that detergent box.
Instead, turn it into a cheerful storage bin.**

Design by Heidi Borchers, SCD

Materials

Clean, empty detergent box
Knife
½ yard star fabric
Aleene's Fusible Web™
Aleene's Ultimate Glue Gun™
Aleene's All Purpose Glue Sticks™
2" x 8½" piece felt
Fabric scraps in desired colors
4" length ¹⁄₁₆"-wide ribbon
Fine-tip permanent black marker
Blush

Directions

Note: See page 6 for tips on working with fusible web.

1 Cut lid from box, using knife. Set aside.

2 From fabric, cut 1 (5" x 8½") piece for inside lid, 1 (8" x 12¾") piece for lid, and 1 (11½" x 34½") piece for box. Fuse web to wrong side of fabric pieces. Remove paper backing from fabric pieces.

3 Place corresponding fabric onto lid, with web side down. Fuse fabric to lid, smoothing edges. If necessary, use glue to anchor corners and let dry. Repeat to fuse fabric pieces to inside lid and to outside of box.

4 For hinge between lid and box, glue felt lengthwise to back edge of inside lid so that 1" extends beyond lid edge. Let dry. Glue felt extension to inside top back edge of box. Let dry.

5 For ballerina design on front of box, transfer patterns to paper side of fusible web. Cut out and fuse to wrong side of desired fabric scraps. Cut out and then fuse designs to front of box in following order: body, dress, hair, and shoes. Tie ribbon in bow and glue to waist. Let dry. Draw eyes and mouth, using black marker. Brush on circles of blush for cheeks.

Body

Hair

Dress

Shoe

Handmade

From birthdays to graduation and Christmas to weddings, a gift made with love is special.

ALEENE'S

FAVORITE

RECIPES

Presents

Toss the Bouquet

Use a heat gun to curl the edges of Satin Sheen™ petals for picture-perfect roses.

Materials
Aleene's Satin Sheen Ribbon™:
    dark green, ivory, yellow
Fine-tip permanent black marker
Pinking shears
Waxed paper
Aleene's Premium-Coat™ Acrylic
    Paints: Light Fuchsia, Deep
    Spruce, Black
½"-wide flat paintbrush
Heat gun
Aleene's Thick Designer Tacky
    Glue™
Wire: 18-gauge, 22-gauge
Green florist's tape
3"-diameter foam ball
Green moss
Ribbons: 3 to 4 yards 1½"-wide,
    1 to 2 yards ½"-wide
Filler flowers, such as small silk
    blossoms, preserved ferns,
    baby's breath

Directions

Note: This bouquet has 3 roses, 4 rosebuds, 2 tight rosebuds, 3 lilies, and 15 leaves. Adapt directions to make desired size bouquet.

1 Flatten each color of Satin Sheen. From dark green, cut 3½" lengths for leaves; each length yields 3 to 4 leaves. From ivory, cut 3½" lengths for rose petals; each length yields 2 rose petals. (Tight rose bud requires 2 petals, looser bud requires 3 or 4 petals, and full rose requires 8 to 12 petals.) From ivory, cut 4" lengths for lilies; each length yields 3 lily petals. (Lily requires 4 to 6 petals.) Using permanent marker and following patterns on page 44, trace petals and leaves onto Satin Sheen lengths. Cut out (use pinking shears to cut out leaves). For each lily, trace 1 lily center onto yellow Satin Sheen and cut out.

2 Place petals onto piece of waxed paper. Pour small puddle of Light Fuchsia onto another piece of waxed paper and add small amount of water to create wash. Using paintbrush, apply wash to edges and sides of rose and lily petals (see photo). Let dry. Then pour small puddle of Deep Spruce and add water to create wash. Brush Deep Spruce wash on inside center of lily petals (see photo). Let dry. Then pour small puddle of Black. Brush undiluted Black onto top edges of lily centers (see photo). Let dry.

3 To curl edges of rose petals, direct heat from heat gun at back top edge of each petal, working with one at a time. (Since Satin Sheen curls quickly, do not overheat.) Let cool.

4 **For roses and rosebuds,** working with 1 petal at a time, place glue on petal as shown on pattern. Roll first petal tightly. Add glue to another petal and roll around first petal. Continue adding petals, rolling each added petal more loosely than petal before it, until rose or bud is desired size. Let dry. Using 22-gauge wire and referring to Wiring Diagram on page 44, wrap petals together at base of each flower or bud; leave 1"-length of wire extending from cover wire with florist's tape.

5 **For lilies,** place glue along bottom edge of 1 lily center and pinch together. Let dry. Heat tip of center with heat gun to curl slightly. Let cool. Working with 1 petal at a time, place glue on petal as shown on pattern, pinch lower edge, and shape around center (see photo). Add petals until lily is desired size. Let dry. Using 22-gauge wire, wrap

petals together at base of each lily; leave 1"-length of wire extending from flower for stem. At base of flower, cover wire with florist's tape.

6 Use heat gun to heat edge of each leaf until it curls slightly. Use florist's tape to attach each leaf to flower or stem as desired (see photo on page 42). If desired, tape 2½" length of 22-gauge wire to leaf (to insert directly into foam ball).

7 To assemble bouquet, cut 14" length of 18-gauge wire. Bend in half and dip ends into glue. Insert ends into foam ball. Let dry. Wrap exposed length of wire with florist's tape and bend into comfortable position for carrying. Cover foam ball with glue. Press moss into glue. Let dry. Dip flower stems and leaf stems into glue and insert into foam ball as desired. Let dry. Make bow from 1½"-wide ribbon and glue in place on bouquet. Let dry. Cut ½"-wide ribbon into 12" lengths. Form each length into loop and glue in place on bouquet. Let dry. Glue filler flowers in bouquet as desired. Let dry.

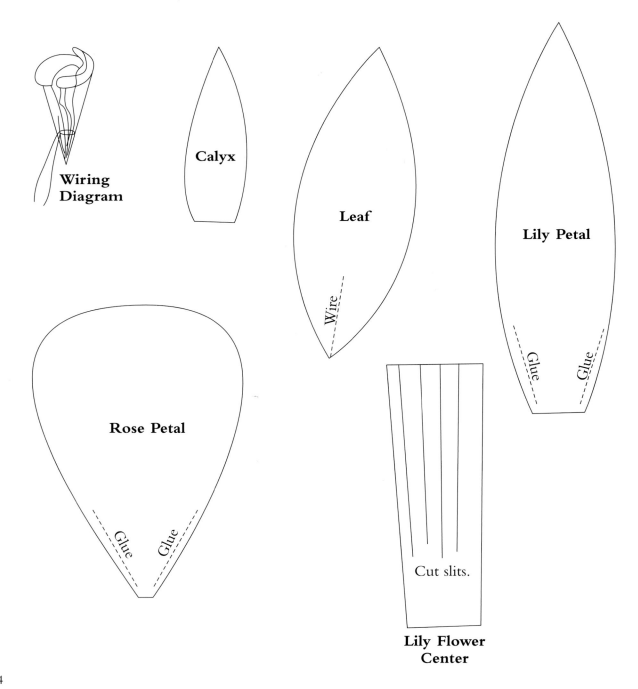

Wiring Diagram

Calyx

Leaf

Wire

Lily Petal

Glue   Glue

Rose Petal

Glue   Glue

Cut slits.

Lily Flower Center

Rx for the Road

Decorate the front of this auto first-aid kit with maps of the gift recipient's hometown, and he or she will have an extra reason to keep it handy.

Materials
Assorted maps
Aleene's CraftKeeper™ Custom Fit Organizer
1" flat paintbrush
Aleene's Instant Decoupage™: gloss
Aleene's Enhancers™: Gloss Varnish
¼"-wide felt-tip permanent red marker
Assorted first-aid items

Directions

1 Cut maps to fit top and sides of box, rounding corners to match box shape. (If gift recipient is taking a trip, use maps of that area.) Then cut piece for back of box, notching paper at hinges.

2 Brush 1 coat of Instant Decoupage on 1 side of box and on back of corresponding map piece. Press map piece in place. Smooth out any wrinkles and bubbles, using fingers. Brush 1 coat of Instant Decoupage over map. Let dry. Repeat with remaining pieces to cover entire box.

3 Brush 1 coat of Gloss Varnish on entire box. Let dry. Using red marker, write "First Aid" and draw red cross on front of box (see photo). Fill with supplies.

Design by Cheryl Ball, SCD

Cookbook CAPERS

Decoupage the cover of a photo album, fill it with your favorite recipes, and give it to a new graduate or a newlywed.

Materials

Aleene's Premium-Coat™ Acrylic Paints: Dusty Sage, Soft Sand
3-ring magnetic photo album
1½" square sponge
Paper (slightly heavier than typing paper)
Rub-on letters to personalize
Aleene's Decoupage Print™: Table Top Setting
Aleene's Instant Decoupage™
Aleene's Paper Napkin Appliqué Glue™
Divider tabs

Directions

Note: To personalize cookbook, you can use a computer to print desired words directly onto paper (see Step 2).

1 Sponge Dusty Sage onto photo album cover. Let dry. Sponge Soft Sand randomly over Dusty Sage (see photo). Let dry.

2 To personalize cookbook, lightly sponge-paint paper to match album cover. Let dry. Print desired words onto paper using rub-on letters. Cut as desired to fit on album.

3 Cut desired designs from decoupage prints (see photo for inspiration). Brush 1 coat of Instant Decoupage where desired on album cover; then brush 1 coat on back of desired cutout. Position cutout on album. Smooth out any wrinkles and bubbles, using fingers. Then brush additional coat over cutout. Repeat as desired with cutouts and personalized lettering. Let dry.

4 For waterproof protective finish, brush appliqué glue over entire album. Let dry.

Insert divider tabs into book. For extra gift, include some of your favorite recipes.

Design by Joan Fee, SCD

Funky and Functional

Beads, wire, and opaque markers decorate a Shrink-It™ candleholder.

Materials
Aleene's Shrink-It™: 5 sheets clear, 1 sheet Opake
Hole punch
Aleene's Baking Board or non-stick cookie sheet, sprinkled with baby powder
Wire cooling rack
Permanent opaque markers: white, gold
Copper wire
Wire cutters
Aleene's Crafting Tools™: 4½" diagonal plier, 5" long-nose plier, 5" flat-nose plier
Beads in desired colors and sizes
3 votive candles

Directions

Note: See page 7 for tips on working with Shrink-It.

1 Punch 1 hole in each corner of 1 clear Shrink-It sheet; then punch 2 holes each in center of 3 sides of clear sheet. (Sides without holes will be at top of candleholder.) Repeat with 3 more clear Shrink-It sheets. With remaining clear sheet (bottom of candleholder), punch 1 hole in each corner and 2 holes in center of each side.

2 Using pencil, trace star pattern 4 times onto Opake Shrink-It sheet. Cut out and punch 1 hole in top of each star.

3 Preheat toaster oven or conventional oven to 250°. Working with 1 sheet at a time, place on room-temperature baking board and cover with wire rack to prevent Shrink-It from curling. Place sheet in oven. Remove when sheet is completely flat. Repeat to shrink all sheets and Shrink-It stars, omitting wire rack when shrinking stars. Let cool. Use white opaque pen to draw stars, suns, and other shapes on Shrink-It as desired (see photo). Outline stars, using gold opaque pen.

4 From copper wire, cut 16 (6") lengths. Using Crafting Tools as needed, thread 1 wire through matched holes at 1 top corner and twist wire to secure (see photo). Repeat at remaining top corners; then wire sides together in centers of sheets. Finally, wire sides and bottom together at corners and then attach at center of sheets. Add beads and stars as desired and curl wires into decorative shapes (see photo).

5 For hanger, cut 3 pieces of copper wire to desired length; cut another piece about 6" longer. Attach 1 piece of wire to each corner of candleholder. Twist all 4 wires together where shorter ones meet above candleholder and add decorative beads (see photo). Then shape end of longer wire to form hanger. Place votive candles into candleholder. Do not leave unattended while candles are lit.

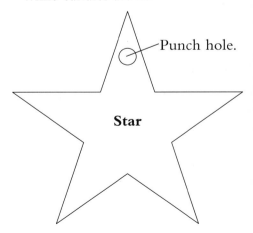

Punch hole.

Star

Psychedelic Screen Frame

Please a teenager on your gift list with a reversible computer screen accessory.

Materials

Aleene's Premium-Coat™ Acrylic Paints: White, Light Fuchsia, Light Turquoise
Paintbrush
Wooden computer screen cover (available from crafts and hobby stores)
2 wooden craft sticks
Aleene's Decoupage Prints™: Mystery Spill
Decorative-edge scissors
Aleene's Instant Decoupage™: Gloss
Tulip Dimensional Paints: Snow White Pearl, Orange Pearl, Peppermint Pearl, and Heather Pearl for orange side; Blue Pearl, Snow White Pearl, Sea Mist, and Slick Teal for green side
Aleene's Enhancers™: Gloss Varnish
Adhesive-backed hook-and-loop tape

Directions

1 Paint outside and inside edge of cover White. Let dry. Paint 1 side Light Fuchsia. Let dry. Paint remaining side Light Turquoise. Let dry. Paint sides and edges of 1 craft stick Light Fuchsia; paint remaining craft stick Light Turquoise. Let dry.

2 Trace cover onto decoupage print 1 time in orange area and 1 time in green area; cut out so that print fits just inside cover, using decorative-edge scissors. (Piece orange side to fit cover; match pattern as much as possible.)

3 Working on small sections at a time, brush 1 coat of Instant Decoupage onto wood and back of 1 print. Position print on cover and smooth out any wrinkles or bubbles, using fingers. Then brush another coat of Instant Decoupage over print. Let dry. Repeat to apply remaining print to remaining side of cover.

4 Using dimensional paints, add details to 1 side of screen cover (see photos). Let dry. Repeat on remaining side of cover. Paint desired name on 1 side of each craft stick. Let dry. Apply 1 coat varnish to each side of cover and to craft sticks, letting 1 side dry before turning over.

5 Cut hook-and-loop tape into 3 pieces, each 1" shorter than craft stick. Peel backing from loop side of 1 hook-and-loop tape piece and stick to top center of computer above screen. Center cover on computer screen and stick hook half of hook-and-loop tape to cover. Stick hook half of another hook-and-loop tape piece to reverse of cover in same position. Stick loop half of 1 hook-and-loop tape piece to back of each craft stick. Discard remaining hook piece of hook-and-loop tape. Use craft stick/nameplate to cover hook-and-loop tape on exposed side.

Design by Cheryl Ball, SCD

Graduation Day

Adorn cupcakes, keychains, picture frames, gifts, and more with miniature mortarboards.

Materials

For each: **Aleene's Shrink-It™ Opake**
¼" hole punch
Aleene's Baking Board or non-stick cookie sheet, sprinkled with baby powder
1"-diameter thread spool
Aleene's Ultimate Glue Gun™
Aleene's All-purpose Glue Sticks™
Aleene's Premium-Coat™ Acrylic Paints: Black or school colors (optional)
#10 shader paintbrush
Fine-tip permanent black marker (optional)
For keychain: **Desired keychain**
For garland: **Star garland in black and white**
Needlenose pliers
Jump rings
For picture frame: **Desired picture frame**
For place cards: **Desired number of blank place cards**

Directions

Note: See page 7 for tips on working with Shrink-It.

1 **For keychain or garland,** cut 1 (4") square from Shrink-It for top of each desired mortarboard, 1 (1¾" x 8¼") piece for each mortarboard band, and 1 (¹⁄₁₆" x 3") piece for each tassel string. Punch hole at 1 corner of each mortarboard top. Then cut 1 (¼" x ¾") piece for each tassel and cut ½" slits every ¹⁄₁₆" along ¼" edge of each to make fringe; round corners on unfringed edge of tassel.

2 **For picture frame or each place card,** cut 1 (4") square from Shrink-It for top of mortarboard and then cut square in half diagonally (makes 2 miniature mortarboard decorations). Cut 1¾" x 4" piece for each mortarboard band. See Step 1 to cut tassel string and to cut and fringe tassel.

3 Preheat toaster oven or conventional oven to 250°. Place Shrink-It designs on room-temperature baking board and bake in oven. Remove from oven and, while Shrink-It is still warm, roll each band around spool to shape; slip off end of spool. Place 1 end of warm tassel string at center of square and drape excess over edge. Hold band and tassel string in place until cool. (If Shrink-It pieces harden too quickly, place back into oven and reshape while warm.) Glue 1 band to bottom of each mortarboard top; glue tassel string to center of top and glue tassel to end of tassel string. Let dry.

4 Paint each mortarboard Black or with school colors, if desired. Let dry. Use permanent marker to write school name, graduate's name, or year on unpainted mortarboard top, if desired. **For keychain,** thread attachment through hole in mortarboard top. **For garland,** use pliers to attach 1 jump ring through hole in each mortarboard top and then attach jump ring to garland. **For picture frame or each place card,** glue half-mortarboards to object as desired; let dry.

Velvet and Roses

Materials
1½ yards 1"-wide green velvet
   ribbon
Aleene's Thick Designer Tacky
   Glue™
8" x 10" wooden frame
1 yard rose floral trim
Aleene's Botanical Preserved
   Flowers and Foliage™: 12 Rosa
   "Mercedes" Red
Lace photo mat

Directions
Cut ribbon into 2 (10") lengths and 2 (12") lengths. Glue ribbon lengths to corresponding sides of frame, folding cut ends to back. Let dry. Glue 1 length of floral trim along center of each ribbon piece (see photo). Let dry. Remove dried roses from stems. Glue in clusters of 3 in each corner. Let dry. Remove glass from frame and center lace mat over photo. Glue mat to edges of photo. Let dry. Place matted picture back in frame.

Display a family photo elegantly with velvet ribbon, dried roses, and a lace mat.

Design by Katheryn Tidwell Foutz

Time for Ties

Draw a fishing motif on a tie rack to make a practical Father's Day gift.

Materials

6" x 12" wooden towel or tie rack
Fine-grain sandpaper
Tack cloth
Spray clear acrylic sealer
Matte finish cream spray paint
Pencil with eraser
Graphite paper
Evanscraft Pens: Colonial Green, Shadow Green, Christmas Green, Rosy Mauve, and Dark Black finepoint; Colonial Green, Natural Wicker, Sunny Yellow, Chocolate Brown, and Harvest Gold medium-point

Directions

1 Sand entire rack. Wipe with tack cloth to remove dust. Apply several light coats of acrylic sealer, letting dry after each application. Apply 4 coats of cream paint, letting dry between coats.

2 Transfer pattern to wood, using pencil and graphite paper (see photo). Using Colonial Green finepoint, trace lettering. Using medium-point Colonial Green, make dots at ends of letters. Let dry. Erase any excess graphite dust, smears, or lines.

3 Transfer fish and basket to rack, using pencil and graphite paper. Using Evanscraft Pens, fill in designs as follows.

For each fish, using finepoint Colonial Green, Shadow Green, and Christmas Green, lightly stroke along back of fish, tail, and fins, leaving small amount of white spots (see photo). Let dry. Use Shadow Green to outline fish, mouth, gills, fins, and tail. Use Rosy Mauve to fill in stomach, leaving white spots on stomach. Let dry. Color some white spots Natural Wicker and some Sunny Yellow. Touch up any white spots with Natural Wicker. Use Dark Black to add eye and other dots as desired. Let dry.

For basket, using Natural Wicker, fill in basket, leaving some white spaces. Let dry. Fill in white spaces with Sunny Yellow. Use Dark Black to outline basket and panels and Chocolate Brown to paint strap and lid trim. Let dry. Use Harvest Gold to paint buckles. Let dry. Use Dark Black to paint holes on leather and small curved lines to simulate individual wicker pieces (see photo). Let dry.

4 Using medium-point Colonial Green, outline edge of rack. Start at bottom and move slowly and evenly around rack, making sure to stay in groove of wood. Sign and date back of rack.

5 When completely dry, spray rack with several light coats of acrylic sealer, letting dry after each coat.

Design by
Alma Mitchell

Corner to Corner

Working this afghan diagonally offers a new angle on crocheting.

Materials

Worsted-weight Berella "4" yarn by Bernat:
  4 skeins (880 yards or 400 grams) Deep
  Sea Green, 6 skeins (1,110 yards or 510
  grams) Wine Mist Ombre, 4 skeins (880
  yards or 400 grams) Dark Orchid
Crochet hook, size I (9/5.5 mm) or size
  needed to obtain gauge

Finished Size: 48" x 64"
Gauge: 1 sh = 1"

Notes

In afghan pictured, Color A is Deep Sea
Green, Color B is Wine Mist Ombre, and
Color C is Dark Orchid.

Afghan is worked diagonally, from corner
to opposite corner.

Change colors as foll: In last st before
changing to new color, work until 2 lps
remain on hook. With new color, yo and
draw through last 2 lps on hook.

Standard Abbreviations

ch	chain(s)
col	color
cont	continu(e) (ing)
dc	double crochet
ea	each
est	established
foll	follow(s) (ing)
pat	pattern
rep	repeat(s)
sh	shell
sl st	slip stitch
sp(s)	space(s)
st(s)	stitch(es)
yo	yarn over

Design by Bernat for Solutia

Striping Pattern

Rows 1–39: Col A
Row 40: Col B
Rows 41–45: Col A
Rows 46 and 47: Col B
Rows 48–51: Col A
Rows 52–54: Col B
Rows 55–57: Col A
Rows 58–61: Col B
Rows 62 and 63: Col A
Rows 64–68: Col B
Row 69: Col A
Row 70: Col B
Row 71: Col C
Rows 72–76: Col B
Rows 77 and 78: Col C
Rows 79–82: Col B
Rows 83–85: Col C
Rows 86–88: Col B
Rows 89–92: Col C
Rows 93 and 94: Col B
Rows 95–99: Col C
Row 100: Col B
Rows 101–189: Col C

Directions

Using Col A, ch 5. Work foll Striping Pat for col changes.

Row 1: Work 3 dc in 4th st from hook: 1 sh.

Row 2: Ch 5, turn; work 3 dc in 4th st from hook, sl st in 3rd dc of next sh, ch 3, 3 dc under ch sp of same sh: 2 sh.

Row 3: Ch 5, turn; work 3 dc in 4th st from hook, [sl st in 3rd dc of next sh, ch 3, 3 dc under next ch sp of same sh] twice: 3 sh.

Rows 4–60: Cont in Striping Pat, rep Row 3, adding 1 sh in every row until you have 60 sh in a row.

Row 61: Ch 1, turn, sl st in ea dc of first sh, ch 3, work in pat as est to end of row.

Row 62: Ch 5, turn, work in est pat to last sh, sl st in 3rd dc of same sh: 60 sh.

Row 63 and all odd-numbered rows through Row 79: Rep Row 61.

Row 64 and all even-numbered rows through Row 80: Rep Row 62.

Row 81: Cont in Striping Pat, ch 1, turn; sl st in ea dc of first sh, ch 3, work in est pat to last group, sl st in 3rd dc of last sh: 59 sh.

Rows 82–139: Cont in Striping Pat, rep Row 81, which reduces ea row by 1 sh, until 1 sh remains. Fasten off. Weave in all ends.

Helping Hands

Fabric stiffener and polyfill convert garden gloves into clever and attractive gifts.

Designs by Judy Malone

Materials

For each: Polyfill
Aleene's Fabric Stiffener and Draping Liquid™
Aleene's Thick Designer Tacky Glue™
Raffia
For shelf: 2" x 12" wooden board with 2 pegs
Wooden shapes: 1 heart, 1 flower with stem, 5 leaves
Aleene's Enhancers™: All-Purpose Primer, Matte Varnish
Paintbrushes: ¾" flat, stencil, #0 liner, Deerfoot, spatter brush, sponge brush
Sandpaper
Tack cloth
Damp paper towels
Drill with appropriate bit
½" check stencil
Aleene's Premium-Coat™ Acrylic Paints: Soft Sand, Black, True Red, Light Turquoise, Deep Sage, Deep Beige
Aleene's Essentials™: Yellow Ochre, Burnt Umber
Garden tool
Aleene's Premium Designer Brush™: #12 shader

Graphite paper
Permanent black marker
2 (1'-long) Allthread steel rods, size 10-24
Large garden glove
Hacksaw
4 nuts with washers, size 10-24
19-gauge wire
Wire cutters
Pliers
Ivy in 4" pot (optional)
For pincushion: Permanent fabric marking pen (optional)
Plain fabric or ribbon scraps (optional)
Child's glove
Aleene's Fusible Web™ scraps
Assorted buttons
Thread spool
Large print fabric scrap
19-gauge wire
For blooming glove: Large garden glove
Red print fabric scrap
Bee button or charm
Permanent fabric marker
Spanish moss
3 pigeon eggs
Silk flowers and ivy

Directions for shelf

Note: See page 6 for tips on working with fusible web.

1 Remove pegs from board. Apply primer to all wood surfaces, using flat brush. Let dry. Sand lightly. Wipe with tack cloth to remove dust. Drill small holes in top of heart (see photo) and base of each leaf. Drill 1 small hole about 1½" to right of hole left by removed left peg.

2 Paint board and 1 peg Soft Sand, using flat brush. Let dry. Position stencil on board. Pounce Black checks on board, using stencil brush. Let dry. Using flat brush, paint heart True Red, flower Yellow Ochre, tool handle Light Turquoise, and leaves Deep Sage. Let dry.

3 Transfer lettering to heart (see pattern on page 60). Using liner brush, paint lettering Black. Let dry. Using Burnt Umber and Deerfoot brush, stipple flower center (see photo). Let

dry. Using wooden end of paint-brush, paint True Red and Black dots in flower center. Let dry. Use permanent marker to draw veins and to outline leaves and flower petals (see photo). Distress all painted edges, using sandpaper. Wipe with tack cloth to remove dust. Spatter all painted surfaces, using Black and spatter brush. Let dry.

4 Mix 4 parts water with 1 part Burnt Umber and 1 part Deep Beige to create wash. Using flat brush and working on 1 small area at a time, apply wash over all painted surfaces. Wipe with damp paper towel before wash dries. Then let dry. Apply 2 coats of varnish to all painted surfaces, using flat brush. Let dry after each coat.

5 Measure steel rods to fit from end of finger in glove through board, adding enough length to attach rod with nut and washer. Using hacksaw, saw off

excess. Do not attach rods. Place rods in 2 fingers of glove and fill glove with polyfill, molding into desired shape. Using sponge brush, apply fabric stiffener to glove. Shape glove as desired as fabric stiffener dries. Apply additional coats of fabric stiffener as needed to obtain desired firmness, letting dry between coats.

6 Place 1 nut and washer on each rod. Place end of 1 rod through drilled hole in board and end of second rod through left peghole. Bolt in place, using nuts and washers on back of board, too. Glue painted peg into remaining peghole, using Tacky Glue. Let dry. Using flat brush, apply wash to glove (see Step 4 on page 59). Let dry.

7 Cut 16" length of wire. Thread 1 end through each hole in heart. Use pliers to twist and coil ends to secure (see photo on pages 58 and 59) and to shape hanger at top center of wire loop. Tie raffia bow to top of wire below hanger. Use pliers to wire leaves to flower stem (see photo). Glue flower to stem, using Tacky Glue. Let dry. Glue stem to board. Let dry. Tie length of raffia to garden tool and hang from glove (see photo). If desired, place pot of ivy on top of glove.

Directions for pincushion

Note: See page 6 for tips on working with fusible web.

If desired, use permanent fabric marker to write "a stitch in time saves nine" or other saying on ribbon or plain fabric scraps. Fuse scraps to palm of glove (see photo). Overstuff glove with polyfill. Position large fabric scrap on top of glove, tucking edges inside glove at wrist. (Add polyfill if needed.) Glue fabric edges inside glove, using Tacky Glue. Let dry. Stiffen glove as in Step 5 of

directions for shelf. Let dry. Place buttons and spool on wire, twisting wire with pliers as desired to hold buttons and spool in place. Insert ends of wire into glove. Tie raffia bow around wrist of glove.

Directions for blooming glove

Fill glove with polyfill. Stiffen as in Step 5 of directions for shelf. Let dry. Cut heart shape from fabric scrap and glue to palm of glove. Glue or sew bee button to finger of glove (see photo). Let dry. Draw stitching lines around heart, using permanent marker. Glue moss into opening of glove. Let dry. Position eggs in moss; glue flowers and ivy in place. Let dry. Tie raffia in bow and glue to heart (see photo). Let dry. Tie raffia around wrist of glove, leaving long tails. Tie tails into bow for hanger.

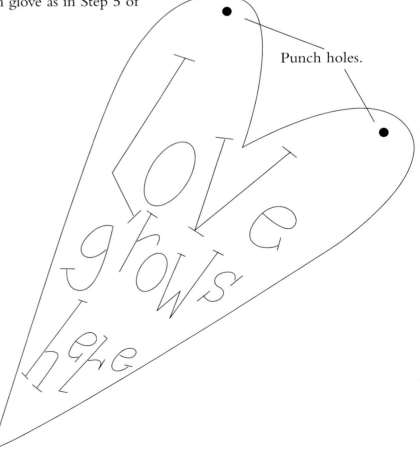

Punch holes.

love grows here

Misty Memories

Use everyday items to give your memory books an original and personalized theme.

Materials
Items to use as stencils, such as
    construction paper, lace,
    doilies, leaves, ribbon,
    feathers, and bits of plastic
Photo album
Airbrush
Airbrush paint in desired colors

Designs by Badger

Directions

1 If using construction paper, tear or cut into desired shapes. Place stencil items on page or album cover as desired, using items singly or in groups.

2 Working 5" to 6" from surface, airbrush desired color. Layer light coats of paint until desired depth of color is achieved. Let dry. Remove stencils.

3 If desired, add other colors to images. For example, feathers in photo above were sprayed with beige and then highlighted with pink. To create soft, pastel borders, spray edges of pages with 1 or more colors. Let dry.

Modern Mosaic Memories

Hot glue and spray paint make these distinctive photo-album covers look like metal.

Designs by Darsee Lett and Pattie Donham

Materials for each album

Artistic Memories Album by Deluxe Craft
Aleene's Ultimate Glue Gun™
Aleene's All-purpose Glue Sticks™
Assorted metal charms, buttons, and beads
Broken pieces of colored glass
Masking tape
Metallic spray paint: copper, gold, or silver
Black spray paint
Damp paper towels (optional)

Directions

1 Disassemble album and set pages aside.

2 Glue charms, buttons, glass, and beads to front of album cover as desired. Let dry. Add lines of glue around each charm, button, glass piece, and bead; fill in blank spaces with lines or curls. Let dry.

3 Cover glass pieces with masking tape. Spray-paint front cover with desired metallic color. Let dry. Spray-paint back cover black. Let dry. For antiqued finish on front cover, spray-paint black over metallic paint in small sections and wipe paint away, using damp paper towels. Let dry. Remove masking tape. Reassemble album.

REMOTE HIDE-AWAY

If Dad isn't a fisherman, fuse another type of design cut from printed fabric to this no-sew armchair caddy.

Materials

1⅓ yards Aleene's Fusible Web™
Fabrics: ½ yard brown striped for pocket; 2" x 3½" piece green broadcloth for fish back; 2½" x 3" piece muslin for fish body; 2½" x 4½" piece heavy white for water splash; 1½" x 3" piece royal blue for water; 3" square spring green broadcloth for fish head and fins
Silver DecorColor™ extrafine paint pen
3" square polyester high-loft batting
Upholstering twist pins (optional)

Directions

Note: See page 6 for tips on working with fusible web. Finished caddy is 8" x 24". If you need longer caddy to hang over your chair arm, adjust length of largest fabric and fusible web rectangles as needed.

1 From fusible web, cut 1 (16" x 24") rectangle and enough 1"-wide strips to equal 128" in length. Transfer patterns to paper side of remaining fusible web and cut out.

2 From pocket fabric, cut 1 (16" x 24") rectangle. Fuse fusible web rectangle to wrong side of fabric rectangle. Remove paper backing. Fold 24" sides into center, with fusible sides together. Fuse to make 8" x 24" rectangle. From remaining pocket fabric, cut 2 (10") squares. Fuse 1" strips

to opposite sides of each square on wrong side of fabric. Remove paper backing, fold fabric under 1", and fuse to make side hems. Then fuse 1" strips to unhemmed edges. Remove paper backing, fold fabric under 1", and fuse to make top and bottom hems. Fuse 1" strips to 3 sides of each square. Remove paper backing. Working with 1 square at a time, position square right side up on 1 end of 8" x 24" fabric piece (see photos). Fuse in place to make pocket.

3 Fuse web patterns to wrong side of appropriate fabrics

and cut out. Cut batting ⅜" smaller than fish body and fuse to back of fish body. Fuse pattern pieces to front of 1 pocket in following order: large fin, upper fin, lower fin, fish body, fish back, fish head, middle fin, water splash, and water. Use silver pen to transfer eye, mouth, and other markings from pattern to muslin fish. Add other details as desired (see photos).

When caddy is complete, use twist pins to attach caddy to arm of chair, if desired.

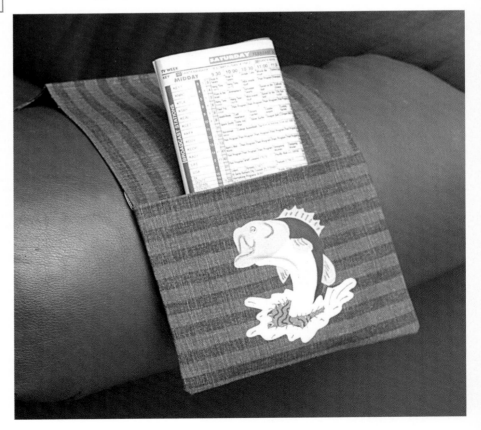

*Design by
Hancock
Fabrics*

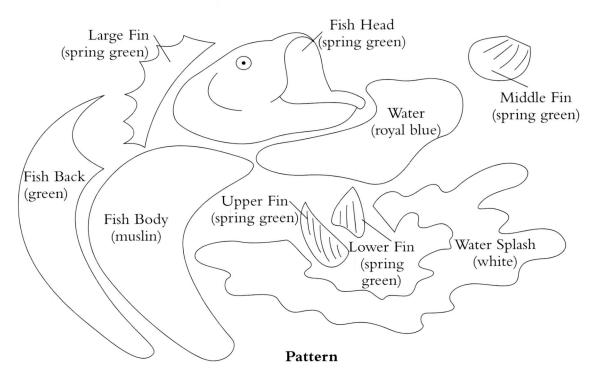

Pattern

Baby Blocks

Simplify a parent's chores with this convenient and decorative organizer.

Designs by Cheryl Ball, SCD

Materials

Aleene's Enhancers™: All-Purpose Primer, Satin Varnish
1" flat paintbrush
Wooden tray
Wooden knobs: 2 (1"), 4 (2")
Sanding sponge
Tack cloth
Aleene's Premium-Coat™ Acrylic Paints: Light Pink, Light Blue, Light Green, Light Yellow, White
Cotton swabs
Wrapping paper
Aleene's Instant Decoupage™: gloss
Decorative-edge scissors
Memory album paper to match wrapping paper
Papier-mâché boxes: 1 (3"-wide), 1 (4"-wide)
Plastic jar
White Scribbles® 3D Paint®
Scribbles® Wide-Liner Tip
Aleene's Thick Designer Tacky Glue™
1 package medium rickrack

Directions

1 Apply 1 coat of primer to all wood surfaces, using flat paintbrush. Let dry. Sand lightly. Wipe with tack cloth to remove dust. Paint inside of tray, 1 small knob, all 4 large knobs, and small box (excluding lid) Light Pink. Let dry. Paint large box lid and outside of handle ends of tray Light Blue. Let dry. Paint small box lid and remaining sides of tray Light Green. Let dry. Paint outside of large box Light Yellow. Let dry. Using cotton swabs and White, paint dots on large knobs, inside of tray, and outside handle ends of tray (see photo at left). Let dry.

2 Cut wrapping paper slightly larger than inside of tray. Lay paper inside tray and run fingernail along edges to form creases. Cut paper along creases. Working on small area at a time, brush 1 coat of Instant Decoupage on inside of tray. Position paper inside tray and smooth out any wrinkles and bubbles, using fingers. Brush another coat of Instant Decoupage over paper. Let dry. From remaining wrapping paper, cut pieces to fit sides and lids of boxes, using decorative-edge scissors. Glue in place as above. Let dry.

3 Cut 6 (1½") squares from memory-album paper, using decorative-edge scissors. Arrange in overlapping random pattern (see photo at left). Adhere to sides of tray, using Instant Decoupage as above. Let dry. From remaining memory-album paper, cut pieces to fit around jar. Adhere with Instant Decoupage as above. Let dry.

4 Remove cap from Scribbles paint and replace with Wide-Liner Tip. Using Scribbles paint, draw letters on boxes and sides of tray as desired. Let dry.

5 Apply 1 or 2 coats of varnish to all pieces. Let dry. Glue large knobs to bottom of tray. Let dry. Glue small knobs to box lids. Let dry. Glue rickrack around tray edges, box lid edges, and edge of jar. Let dry.

String-a-Longs

Spools of thread or twine become individualized accents when decorated with items special to the gift recipient.

Materials

For each: Small piece craft foam
Aleene's Tacky Glue™
Silk greenery picks
For teacher string-a-long: Ball of jute
Wooden ruler
Pencils
Crayons
1 yard ribbon with ruler design
Apple button
For crafty string-a-long: Ball of crochet thread
Knitting needles
Wooden spools
Skeins floss
Assorted buttons
Needles and pins
3"-diameter wooden hoop
Tape measure
1 yard ribbon
For garden string-a-long: Ball of colored twine
Miniature garden gloves
Miniature silk or plastic vegetables

Directions

For teacher string-a-long, remove about 6 yards of jute from center of spool and set aside for another use. **For each,** fill opening of ball with foam. Glue greenery pick in place and shape as desired (see photos). Let dry. Fill in around greenery with appropriate novelty items and glue in place. Let dry. **For teacher string-a-long or crafty string-a-long,** tie ribbon in bow and glue in place (see photos). Let dry.

Teacher String-a-Long

68

Garden String-a-Long

Crafty String-a-Long

Here Fishie, Fishie

Felt fish are ideal for a child's birthday party game or a year-round toy.

Design by Hancock Fabrics

Materials
1¼" yards Aleene's Hot Stitch Paper-Backed Fusible Web™
Felt squares: 1 each of 10 different bright colors, 1 white, 2 black
Disappearing-ink marker
½ yard polyester fleece
15" length black hook-and-loop tape
Aleene's Ultimate Glue Gun™
Aleene's All-Purpose Glue Sticks™
25 (12") red chenille stems
Brown 2" bias tape
Aleene's Fabric Stiffener™
Bowl
1½ yards ⅜" cording
1" x 6" piece gray broadcloth
2 small glue-on wiggle eyes

Directions

Note: See page 6 for tips on working with fusible web.

1 Transfer fish pattern along solid outer line to fusible web 10 times and cut out. Fuse 1 fish on each bright-colored felt square, leaving room on square to cut another fish. Cut out. Do not remove paper backing. Using felt fish as pattern, cut 1 more fish from each color. Match same-color fish piece and mark wrong side of each fish, using disappearing-ink marker.

2 Transfer pattern pieces A and B to fusible web 20 times each and cut out. Fuse As to white felt and Bs to black felt. Cut out. Do not remove paper backing. Transfer numbers 1 through 10 to fusible web twice each. (See page 72. For 9, turn 6 pattern upside down.)

Fuse numbers to black felt. Cut out. Do not remove paper backing.

3 Remove paper backing and fuse 1 black B to right side of each fish (see photo). Repeat to fuse 1 white A to each B and 1 number to each fish. Be sure to fuse same number to each of same-colored fish.

4 From fleece, cut 10 fish, using dashed line on pattern as cutting line. Remove paper backing from web on 1 felt fish and center 1 fleece fish on web wide of felt fish. Place same-colored felt fish on top, matching edges of felt, and fuse together along edges. Repeat to make 10 padded fish.

5 Cut 10 (1½") lengths of hook side of hook-and-loop tape. For each fish, fold 1 length in half and glue to fish for mouth (see pattern for placement). Cut 1 chenille stem in half and set aside. Divide remaining stems into 2 equal bundles. Overlap ends of bundles by 4" (see Pole Diagram) and twist ends together at center to form 20"-long pole.

6 Pour fabric stiffener into bowl and dip bias tape into it, coating both sides. Draw tape through fingers to wipe off excess fabric stiffener. Starting at 1 end of pole, wrap bias tape over ends and up and down pole, overlapping tape slightly, until you use all of tape. Tack or glue ends into fold. Let dry. Loosely wrap 30" of cording around 1 end of pole, leaving remaining cording loose to make fishing line. Wrap broadcloth strip around end of line, overlapping long edges and gluing in place to secure (see photo). Let dry. Dip fabric end of line into fabric stiffener to saturate. Remove excess stiffener, shape into hook, and lay flat to dry.

7 Twist 1 chenille stem half around hook for worm (see photo). Glue wiggle eyes on worm. Let dry. Glue 1" length of loop-side of hook-and-loop tape to bottom of hook. Let dry.

Note: To play, place felt fish in barrel, cooler, or other large container. Let children try to "hook" fish, using pole. To make game more challenging, have children hook fish in numerical order or specify which color each child is supposed to hook.

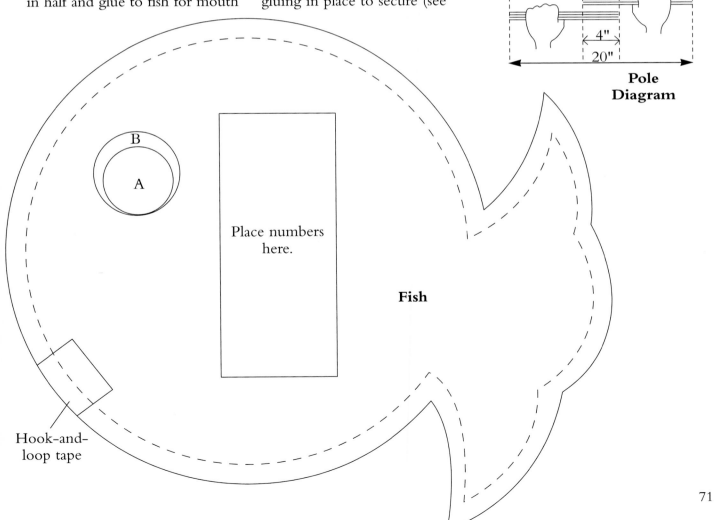

Pole Diagram

4"

20"

B

A

Place numbers here.

Fish

Hook-and-loop tape

Memory Wreath

What better way to honor a special anniversary than with a wreath that features treasured photos.

Materials
Decorative-edge scissors
Photos or color photocopies
Aleene's Decoupage Papers™:
   Whispers of Love
Permanent marker or rub-on
   letters
Archival glue
1½ yards 2"-wide sheer floral
   ribbon
Aleene's Botanical Preserved
   Flowers and Foliage™: German
   Statice/Salal Mixed Natural
   Wreath
Aleene's Ultimate Glue Gun™
Aleene's All-Purpose Glue Sticks™

Directions

Using plain or decorative-edge scissors, cut photos or photocopies to desired size. Cut decoupage paper into pieces slightly larger than photos; then cut piece of decoupage paper and use permanent marker or rub-on letters to add saying as desired (see photo). Glue 1 piece of decoupage paper to back of each corresponding photo, using archival glue. Let dry.

Tie ribbon in double-loop bow. Glue to top center of wreath, using glue gun; do not glue streamers in place. Glue saying over center of bow, using glue gun. Let dry.

Glue photos in place as desired and ribbon streamers around photos, using glue gun (see photo). Let dry.

Design by Joan Fee, SCD

Design by Lee Riggins-Hartman, CCD, CPD, CPT

Silver & Gold

Glitter paint gives plain cosmetic organizers a face lift.

Materials

Plain cosmetic organizer set (We used frosted-glass set with tray, mirror, atomizer, jar, and matching makeup brushes.)
Lint-free cloth
Crayon in any color (optional)
Tulip® 3D Paints™: Liquid Pearl, Gold Glitter, Silver Glitter
3D Paint Design® Tools: Tri-liner TIP, Design Tool (optional)
T-pin or large safety pin
Waxed paper
½" flat soft paintbrush
3D Paint® Sealer: Matte

Directions

1 Thoroughly clean items to be painted and wipe dry with lint-free cloth. If desired, use crayon to sketch designs lightly on each item; when possible, place pattern inside or underneath item and trace designs. Refer to photo for inspiration or use your own creativity.

2 Working on 1 side of item at a time, apply 3D paints to create patterns. Squeeze on scrolls, swirls, dots, or desired designs. For fleur-de-lis, paint teardrops with Gold Glitter and then add dots with Liquid Pearl (see photo). Use Design Tool as desired to pull paint to small points. For other accents, use Tri-Liner TIP with Silver Glitter. Let paint dry for 2 to 3 hours. Turn item and repeat to paint other sides. If side with dry paint will be against work surface, place waxed paper under them to protect painted areas. When finished with all sides, let dry at least 72 hours.

3 Use flat brush to apply coat of Matte Sealer. If decorating a mirror, apply sealer to decorative parts of mirror only. Let dry.

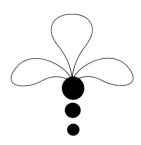

Fleur-de-lis

Swirls

Fashion

Use the simple techniques in this chapter to turn T-shirts, sweatshirts, and other purchased garments into wearable art.

Page 88

Page 90

Magic

Design by Cheryl Ball, SCD

Spring Fever

Easy watercolor designs make an irresistible big shirt.

Materials
Purchased cotton-blend shirt
Cardboard covered with waxed
   paper
Disappearing-ink pen
Aleene's Budget School Glue™
Paper towels
Aleene's Premium-Coat™ Acrylic
   Paints: True Red, True Orange,
   True Yellow, True Green, True
   Turquoise, Light Blue, True
   Violet, True Fuchsia, White
Disposable plastic cups
Paintbrushes: ½" flat, 1" flat
Hair dryer
Soft scrub brush (optional)
Tulip® Dimensional Paint Slick®:
   Medium Blue, Black
Tulip® Dimensional Paint Pearl®:
   Peppermint Pink
3 yards daisy trim
Aleene's OK To Wash-It™ Glue
Daisy appliqués: 4 large, 3 small

Directions
1 Wash and dry shirt. Do not use fabric softener in washing machine or in dryer. Iron as needed to remove wrinkles. Place shirt on cardboard covered with waxed paper and transfer patterns, using disappearing-ink pen (see right and on pages 80 and 81). Adjust sizes of flowers and leaves as needed to fit your shirt (see photo for inspiration).

2 Squeeze thin lines of School Glue over pattern lines, being careful to prevent gaps. (Touch tip of glue bottle to shirt to control flow; line of glue will widen as it dries. Glue lines will help keep paint colors from bleeding outside pattern areas on shirt.) Let dry until glue is clear. Lift shirt as it dries to keep it from sticking to cardboard.

3 Place paper towels between shirt and cardboard. To use paints, pour puddle of each desired color into separate plastic cup and mix 1 part paint with 5 parts water. Starting at center of design, brush on color as desired, using brush width that best matches width of pattern area. If color starts to seep beyond glue

border, use hair dryer to speed drying and to stop seepage. Let each color dry before adding next one. To make shading near edges of flowers, leaves, stems, and in other areas as desired, brush on undiluted paint. Let dry. Mix 1 part Light Blue with 5 parts water. Using 1" flat brush, paint background (see photo on page 78). Let dry. Remove cardboard.

4 Soak shirt in warm water for 20 minutes to dissolve glue. If needed, use soft scrub brush to remove all traces of glue. Let dry.

5 Add details as desired, using dimensional paints. (We used Peppermint Pink to outline flowers on pocket, sleeves, and collar; Medium Blue to outline remaining flowers and leaves; and Black on bee's stripes, antenna, face, and motion swirl.) Let dry.

6 Cut daisy trim to fit shirt placket, skipping buttonhole areas, and across pocket. Using OK To Wash-It, glue trim to shirt. Then glue 1 daisy appliqué to center of each painted flower and to point of each collar (see photo). Let dry. Do not wash shirt for at least 1 week. Turn garment wrong side out, wash by hand, and hang to dry.

Father & Son Pullovers

**Rows of single crochet alternate with rows of double crochet
to form these cozy sweaters.**

Design by Solutia

Gauge: 7 sts = 2" in pat with
large hook
4 rows ribbing = 1½" with
small hook

Finished Chest Measurements:
(23½", 28", 32½", 37", 41¾")
[39½", 44", 48½", 53", 57¾"]

Abbreviations

beg	beginning
ch	chain
col(s)	color(s)
dc	double crochet
dec	decrease
ea	each
est	established
foll	follow(s) (ing)
inc	increas(e) (ing)
lp(s)	loop(s)
MC	main color
pat	pattern
rem	remain(ing)
rep	repeat(ing)
rs	right side
sc	single crochet
sk	skip
st(s)	stitch(es)
yo	yarn over

Special Stitches

**Back post double crochet
(bpdc):** Work dc around back of
post of next dc by inserting hook
from right to left.

**Front post double crochet
(fpdc):** Work dc around front of
post of next dc by inserting hook
from right to left.

Materials

Note: Directions are written
for boy's sizes (2, 4, 6, 8, 10) and
men's sizes [x-small, small, medium,
large, x-large]. To make pattern
easier to follow, circle numbers
appropriate to size you are making before you begin to crochet.
**Red Heart® worsted-weight yarn,
5-oz skeins: (2, 2, 2, 3, 3)**
[1, 1, 1, 2, 2] skein(s) rust
(MC) [Col A]; (1) [5] skein(s)
dark yellow green (Col A) [MC];
(1) [1, 1, 1, 1, 2] skein(s)
gold (Col B) [Col B]
**Crochet hooks, sizes G/6
(4.25 mm) and I/9 (5.5 mm)
or size needed to obtain gauge**
Yarn needle

Note: Change col as foll: In last st before changing to new col, work until 2 lps rem on hook. With new col, yo and draw through last 2 lps on hook. Carry unused col loosely along top of last row and work over it with col being used.

Box Pattern

Row 1 (rs): With MC, ch 3 (counts as 1 dc), sk first sc, dc in next 2 sc, ★ 2 dc Col A, 5 dc MC; rep from ★ across, ending with 3 dc MC instead of 5; turn.

Row 2: With MC, ch 1, sc in first 3 dc, ★ 3 sc Col B, 5 sc MC; rep from ★ across, ending with 3 sc MC instead of 5; turn.

Row 3: With MC, ch 3, sk first sc, dc in each sc across; turn.

Row 4: With MC, ch 1, sc in each dc across; turn.

Row 5: With MC, ch 3, sk first sc, dc in next 6 sc, ★ 3 dc Col A, 5 dc MC; rep from ★ across, ending with 7 dc MC instead of 5; turn.

Row 6: With MC, ch 1, sc in first 7 dc, ★ 3 dc Col B, 5 dc MC; rep from ★ across, ending with 7 sc MC instead of 5; turn.

Rows 7 and 8: Rep Rows 3 and 4.

Rep Rows 1–8 for Box Pat.

Back

With MC and large hook, ch (43, 51, 59, 67, 76) [71, 79, 87, 95, 103].

Row 1: Dc in 4th ch from hook and in ea ch across; turn: (41, 49, 57, 63, 73) [69, 77, 85, 93, 101] dc.

Row 2: Ch 1, sc in ea st across, turn.

Next Rows: Work in Box pat until piece measures (13", 14", 15", 16", 17") [24", 25", 26", 27", 28"] from beg. Fasten off.

Back Ribbing

With Col A and small hook, work (41, 49, 57, 65, 63) [69, 77, 85, 93, 101] dc evenly across beg ch edge; turn.

Ribbing Row: With (Col B) [Col A], ch 2, ★ bpdc, fpdc; rep from ★ across; turn.

Rep Ribbing Row (once) [twice] more with Col B; then (once) [twice] more with Col A; fasten off.

Front

Work as for back until piece meaures (11", 12", 13", 14", 15") [22", 23", 24", 25", 26"] from beg.

Neck Shaping: Cont in est pat, work across first (12, 15, 19, 22, 26) [22, 26, 30, 33, 37] sts, sk next (17, 19, 19, 21, 21) [25, 25, 25, 27, 27] sts for Front Neck, attach second skein of yarn and work across rem sts. Working both sides at same time, dec 1 st at ea neck edge every row twice: (10, 13, 17, 20, 24) [20, 24, 28, 31, 35] sts ea shoulder.

Work even in pat until piece measures same as Back; fasten off.

Front Ribbing: Work same as for Back Ribbing.

Sleeves (Make 2.)

With MC and large hook, ch (43, 47, 51, 55, 59) [47, 47, 47, 55, 55].

Row 1: Dc in 4th ch from hook and in ea ch across: (41, 45, 49, 53, 57) [45, 45, 45, 53, 53] sts.

Rem Rows: Work in Box Pat, inc 1 st ea end every sc row (0) [9, 11, 13, 11, 13] times: (41, 45, 49, 53, 57) [63, 67, 71, 75, 79] sts. For Boys sizes 4 and 8 only, work 2 more sts in MC at beg and end of Box Pat rows. For all sizes, work even until piece measures (9½", 10½", 11½", 12½", 13½") [17", 18", 19", 19½", 20"] from beg; fasten off.

Finishing

Sew Left shoulder seam.

Neck Ribbing: With Col A and small hook, attach yarn at Right Back Neck and work (21, 23, 23, 25, 25) [29, 29, 29, 31, 31] dc across Back Neck, 8 dc along Left Front Neck, (17, 19, 19, 21, 21) [25, 25, 25, 27, 27] dc along Front Neck, 8 dc along Right Front Neck: (54, 58, 58, 62, 62) [70, 70, 70, 74, 74] sts.

Work (1) [2] Ribbing Rows with Col B, and then work 1 Ribbing Row with Col A; fasten off.

Sew Right Shoulder Seam and Neck Ribbing.

Mark (6", 6½", 7", 7½", 8") [9", 9½", 10", 10½", 11"] down from shoulder seams on Front and Back. Sew sleeves between markers.

Sew side and sleeve seams.

Holly Necklace

Who knew ordinary metal screen could be so ornate?

Materials
Metal screen
Old scissors
Waxed paper
Aleene's Tacky Glue™
Gold spray paint
Green Rub 'n Buff
Necklace bar clasp
22" length ½"-wide open braid
24" length ¹⁄₁₆"-wide green satin ribbon
10 (¼"-diameter) red beads
9 jump rings
Aleene's Crafting Tools™: 5" flat-nose plier

Directions

1 Transfer holly leaf pattern to screen and cut 9, using old scissors. Place leaves on waxed paper and apply glue along edges and through center for veins (see photo). Let dry.

2 Spray-paint leaves gold. Let dry. Lightly apply green paste over glue areas, using fingers. Let dry.

3 Place necklace clasp onto end of braid, following manufacturer's instructions. Tie green ribbon onto open end of braid.

String ribbon through braid for about 7". Add 1 bead onto ribbon; continue threading ribbon and adding beads as desired (see photo). Stop adding beads about 7" from clasp end of braid. Thread ribbon through remainder of braid and tie end of ribbon to end of braid near clasp. If desired, glue knots to secure. Let dry.

4 Open jump rings, using flat-nosed plier. Place 1 jump ring on each holly leaf and then place jump rings through braid. Use plier to close jump rings.

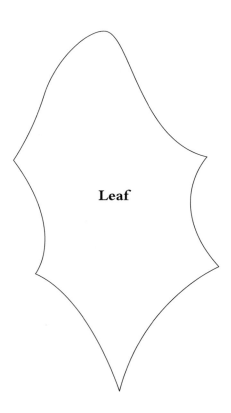

Leaf

The Name Game

A mirror-image technique alters a name into an abstract design for this shirt-and-jacket set.

Materials for each shirt

Purchased sweatshirt or T-shirt
1 (9" x 14½") piece each of 4 coordinating colors of fabric
1 yard Aleene's Hot Stitch Fusible Web™
Embroidery floss to coordinate with shirt color
Large-eyed embroidery needle
Ribbon in coordinating colors (optional)
Assorted buttons

Directions

Note: See page 6 for tips on working with fusible web. You may need extra yardage of web and fabric for very long names or if you plan to make more than 4 names.

1 Wash and dry shirt and fabric; do not use fabric softener in washer or in dryer. Iron as needed to remove wrinkles.

2 **For sweatshirt,** cut open down center front. Fold ¼" to inside along each cut edge and press. From fusible web, cut 2 (¾" x 36") pieces. Fuse 1 strip along inside of 1 folded edge of sweatshirt, covering edge completely. Cut off extended ends of fusible web. Do not remove paper backing. Fold fused edge ¾" to inside, using edge of paper backing as guide. Press lightly. Remove paper backing and fuse. Repeat for remaining cut edge. Using embroidery floss and embroidery needle, make running stitches ⅝" from folded edges of sweatshirt (see photos).

3 **For each,** from fusible web, cut 4 (9" x 14½") pieces. Fuse 1 piece to wrong side of each fabric. Fold each fabric piece in half lengthwise, with right sides together, to make 4½" x 14½" rectangle, with paper backing on outside. On each piece, write name on paper backing, with bottom of writing on fold. If desired, trace child's hand at end of name (see photos). Cut ¼" around writing: cut along traced line of hand.

4 Unfold each name and each hand and then remove paper backing. Position on sweatshirt or T-shirt as desired (see photos). Fuse in place.

5 If desired, tie bows from ribbon. Stitch buttons and bows to shirt, using embroidery floss and embroidery needle (see photos).

Design by Hancock Fabrics

Fl✿wer P✿wer

Pin the Satin Sheen™-and-button flowers to these items so that they're easy to remove for laundering.

Designs by Cheryl Ball, SCD

Materials

For each: **Aleene's Satin Sheen Twisted Ribbon™: True Orange, True Yellow, White**
Lightweight cardboard
1⅛"-diameter covered-button forms (1 for each flower)
Assorted scraps brightly colored fabric
Aleene's Thick Designer Tacky Glue™
½"-diameter brightly colored buttons (1 for each flower)
Purchased shirt, hat, bag, shoes, or other item to decorate
Aleene's Enhancers™: Textile Medium
Aleene's Premium-Coat™ Acrylic Paint: White
Cotton swabs
¾" safety pins (1 for each flower)
For hat: **2 clothespins**
For shoes: **6 brightly colored pony beads**

Directions

1 Untwist Satin Sheen. Transfer petal pattern to cardboard; use cardboard pattern to cut 6 Satin Sheen petals for each flower.

2 Assemble covered buttons, following manufacturer's instructions and using fabric scraps. Glue 6 petals to back of each button, scrunching ends of petals to fit evenly on button. Let dry. Glue 1 button to center front of each covered button (see photo). Let dry.

3 **For hat,** untwist 18" length of True Orange Satin Sheen. Tear lengthwise into 3 equal strips. Braid together. Glue ends together to form loop. Let dry. Place bead of glue along inside edge of hat brim and apply extra glue to glued ends of braid. Slip braid loop over hat brim, with glued ends at bottom center of hat brim; press braid into bead of glue. Hold in place with clothespins until dry. Remove clothespins. (If desired, you can glue flowers to hat instead of pinning them. Let glue dry before wearing.)

4 **For shoes,** tear ½ yard of True Yellow Satin Sheen into strips about 1½" wide. Lace shoes with Satin Sheen strips, threading 1 pony bead between each pair of eyelets.

5 **For each,** mix 1 part Textile Medium and 1 part White paint. Use cotton swab to paint random dots over item where desired. Let dry.

6 Attach flowers to item as desired, using safety pins. Remove flowers before washing item.

Petal

Bunny Blouse

Chenille, doilies, and fabric yo-yos bring spring to a sweatshirt.

Materials for each shirt
Purchased white sweatshirt in child or adult size
Wimpole Street Creations 18" x 30" pink Knobby Chenille Cut
Battenberg doilies
Wimpole Street Creations appliqués: 3 small tulips, 2 large tulips, 2 small Battenberg roses, 2 leaf clusters
Large pastel fabric yo-yos
Aleene's Hot Stitch Fusible Web™
¼"-wide fusible tape
1 yard ¼"-wide seafoam green grosgrain ribbon
Iron-on liquid fusible web
Aleene's OK To Wash-It™ Glue
White minirickrack
White sewing thread
White buttons: 3 (¼") for child's shirt, 1 (½") for adult's shirt
White embroidery floss
Large-eyed embroidery needle

Directions
Note: See page 6 for tips on working with fusible web.

1 Wash and dry sweatshirt, chenille, and doilies; do not use fabric softener in washer or dryer. Iron as needed to remove wrinkles.

2 Cut sleeve and waist ribbing from sweatshirt to desired length. Pin 1" hem along bottom of shirt; topstitch or fuse in place.

3 Cut 1 (3"-wide) strip of chenille long enough to fit around bottom edge of each sleeve plus ½". Sew ends together, using ¼" seam allowance. With edges and seams aligned, place cuff inside sleeve with right side of cuff facing wrong side of sleeve. Pin in place; stitch ¼" seam along lower edge of sleeve through cuff. Turn cuff to outside. Turn raw edge of cuff under ¼" and topstitch to sleeve. Topstitch ¼" from bottom edge of cuff. Repeat for remaining sleeve.

4 Transfer desired bunny pattern to paper side of fusible web. **For child's sweatshirt,** transfer

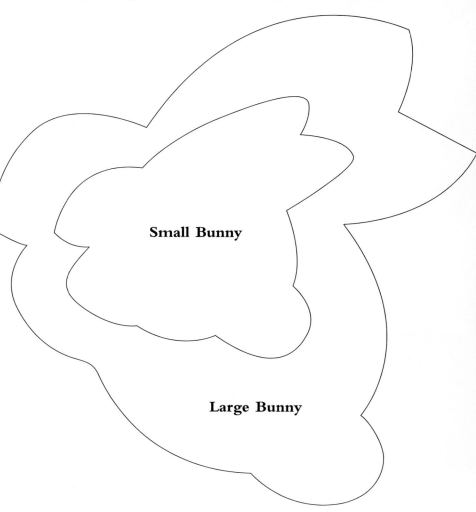

Small Bunny

Large Bunny

3 small bunnies, **For adult sweat-shirt,** transfer 1 large bunny. **For each,** roughly cut out shapes. Fuse bunnies to chenille, arranging so that lines of chenille run diagonally across each bunny. Cut out. Do not remove paper backing. Fuse tape to back of ribbon. Cut apart 1 leaf cluster.

5 Position bunnies, flowers, and leaves on front of sweatshirt as desired. Cut ribbon to desired lengths for flower stems. Fuse stems in place first; then use liquid fusible web to attach lace leaves and flowers. Let dry. Using OK To Wash-It Glue, attach yo-yo flowers. Let dry. Fuse bunnies in place.

6 Position rickrack around outside edge of each bunny. Zigzag in place, using sewing machine. Sew 1 button in place for each bunny's eye, using 12 strands of embroidery floss and embroidery needle. Knot floss on right side of shirt and trim floss close to knot.

Design by Wimpole Street

Victorian Vest

This sophisticated style is wonderfully easy to create with fusible web and glue.

Materials

Purchased white, ivory, or denim vest
Aleene's Fusible Web™
Flat lace: ½ yard 6"- to 8"-wide; 1 yard ½"-, 1"-, or 2"-wide
Aleene's OK To Wash-It™ Glue
Straight pins
Cupid or other romantic iron-on transfer (optional)
15 to 18 assorted round or heart-shaped doilies and appliqués made of Battenberg lace, crochet, and cutwork
1 yard rose trim
1½ yards ½"-wide gathered lace
Purchased lace collar
Small ribbon roses: ivory, rose, mauve
Small buttons
3- to 5-mm pearls
Aleene's Jewel-It™ Glue

Directions

Note: See page 6 for tips on working with fusible web. Unless instructed otherwise, use OK To Wash-It Glue.

1 Wash and dry vest; do not use fabric softener in washer or dryer. Iron as needed to remove wrinkles.

2 Fuse web to back of 6"- to 8"-wide flat lace. Remove paper backing. Fuse lace along center of vest back, trimming raw edges of lace at top and turning raw edges at bottom to inside of vest.

3 On vest front, position narrow flat lace around each armhole, starting at shoulder; ease in curves by snipping slightly with scissors. Glue to secure, holding lace in place until dry with straight pins. Let dry slightly before positioning and securing lace around back portion of armhole. Let dry completely. Remove pins.

4 If desired, iron cupid transfer onto vest front, following manufacturer's instructions. Position doilies, appliqués, and rose trim on front and back of vest as desired (see photo at left). Pin in place. Working with 1 item at a time, apply glue to back of item, replace on vest, and smooth out wrinkles or bubbles, using fingers. Let all items dry completely. Glue gathered lace around bottom edge of vest. Let dry. Pin collar to neckline and sew or glue in place. Let dry.

5 Glue ribbon roses where desired. Let dry. Then add buttons and pearls, using Jewel-It Glue. Apply glue to back of each button or pearl and gently press item onto garment. Be sure to use enough glue so that glue comes up around sides of item. Let dry. (Glue dries clear.)

6 Do not wash garment for at least 1 week. Turn garment wrong side out, wash by hand, and hang to dry.

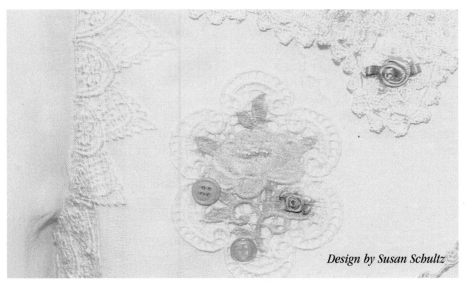

Design by Susan Schultz

WILD THING!

These exotic purses actually began as lunch pails.

Materials for each purse

Lunch pail
Sandpaper
Tack cloth
Vinegar
Aleene's Premium-Coat™ Acrylic
    Paints: Ivory, Black
Aleene's Essentials™: Yellow Ochre,
    Burnt Umber
Aleene's Enhancers™: Flow Medium,
    Matte Varnish
Paintbrushes: 2" sponge, ¾" flat,
    #1 round, #2 round, #0 liner
Paper plate
Sea wool sponge
2 yards black rattail cording
Large-eyed embroidery or tapestry
    needle
Aleene's Thick Designer Tacky
    Glue™
1 yard ¼" black cording
1" black frog closure
1 black tassel

Directions

1 Wash pail with soap and water. Let dry. Sand surfaces. Wipe with tack cloth to remove dust. Rinse pail with vinegar and then with water. Let dry. Paint pail Ivory, using sponge brush. Let dry. If needed, add coats to cover thoroughly, letting dry between coats. Paint hinge Black.

2 **For leopard pattern,** working on 1 side of pail at a time, brush Flow Medium over pail, using flat brush. Let dry. Mix 1 part Yellow Ochre and 4 parts Flow Medium. Brush on mixture, using flat brush. Pour puddle of Yellow Ochre onto paper plate and dip sea sponge into paint. Sponge on dense areas of color (see photo). Let dry. Mix 1 part Burnt Umber and 1 part Flow Medium. Load stencil brush with mixture and pounce various sizes of circles on pail. Let dry. Load #1 round brush with Black; outline Burnt Umber circles and add random black spots (see photo). Let dry. **For zebra pattern,** lightly pencil Vs on lid. Load #2 round brush with Black and paint Vs. Using liner brush, pull small lines out of thick ones (see photo). Let dry. **For each,** apply 1 or 2 coats of varnish, letting dry after each coat.

3 Buttonhole-stitch around handle, using rattail cording and embroidery or tapestry needle. Glue ends in place. Let dry. Cut 1 piece of black cording to fit around lid plus enough to knot each end (see photo). Glue in place, ending with 1 knot on either side of hinge. Let dry. Glue frog to top of hinge. Let dry. Loop tassel around hinge. If needed, cut tassel to same length as pail or shorter.

Designs by Judy Malone

To Dye For

Try the same tie-dye technique used for these garments to make groovy curtains for a teenager's room.

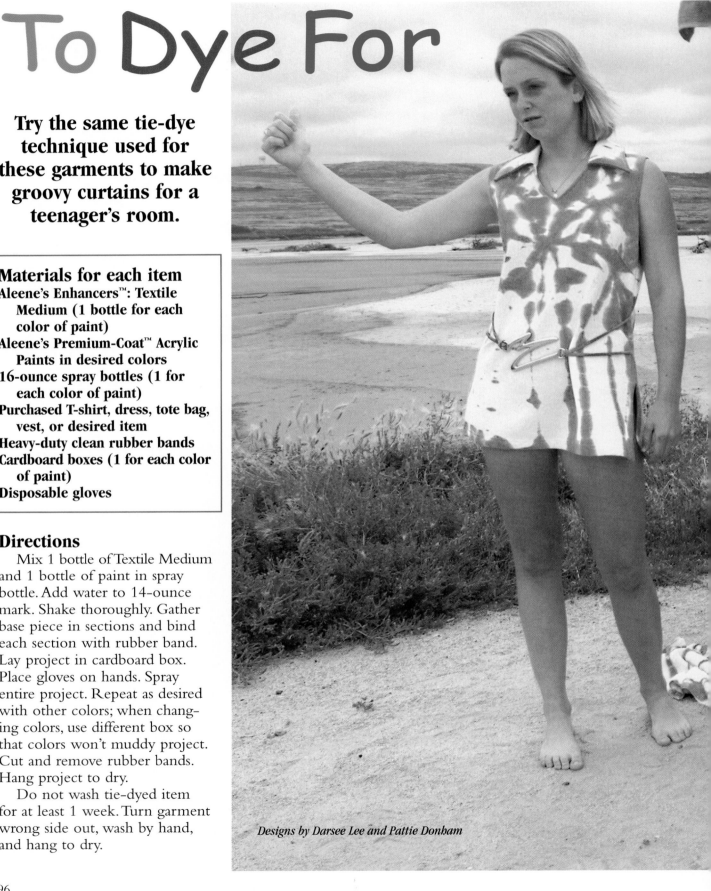

Materials for each item

Aleene's Enhancers™: Textile Medium (1 bottle for each color of paint)

Aleene's Premium-Coat™ Acrylic Paints in desired colors

16-ounce spray bottles (1 for each color of paint)

Purchased T-shirt, dress, tote bag, vest, or desired item

Heavy-duty clean rubber bands

Cardboard boxes (1 for each color of paint)

Disposable gloves

Directions

Mix 1 bottle of Textile Medium and 1 bottle of paint in spray bottle. Add water to 14-ounce mark. Shake thoroughly. Gather base piece in sections and bind each section with rubber band. Lay project in cardboard box. Place gloves on hands. Spray entire project. Repeat as desired with other colors; when changing colors, use different box so that colors won't muddy project. Cut and remove rubber bands. Hang project to dry.

Do not wash tie-dyed item for at least 1 week. Turn garment wrong side out, wash by hand, and hang to dry.

Designs by Darsee Lee and Pattie Donham

This **IS** my costume!

Suit up for Halloween in a jiffy with a T-shirt and tissue paper appliquès.

Design by Joan Fee, SCD

Materials
Purchased light-colored T-shirt
Cardboard covered with waxed paper
Aleene's Crafting Tissue Paper™: True Orange, Burnt Umber, Black
Disappearing-ink pen
Aleene's Paper Napkin Appliqué Glue™
Aleene's Premium Designer Brush™: ½" shader
Dimensional paints: black, green

Directions

1 Wash and dry shirt; do not use fabric softener in washer or dryer. Iron as needed to remove wrinkles. Place cardboard covered with waxed paper inside shirt.

2 Transfer patterns to corresponding tissue paper, using pencil. Cut out inside pencil lines. Position tissue-paper pieces on shirt and trace around each, using disappearing-ink pen. Remove tissue.

3 Apply glue to T-shirt within marked lines, using brush. Replace tissue-paper pumpkin on shirt. Apply 1 coat of glue to front of tissue-paper piece. Let dry. Repeat to glue bats and pumpkin eyes, nose, mouth, and stem.

4 Using disappearing-ink pen, write Happy Halloween on shirt (see photo). Using black paint, trace letters, making squiggly lines (see photo). Let dry. Using black paint, outline jack-'o-lantern and add vertical lines (see photo). Let dry. Using green paint, add dots to make bat eyes. Remove cardboard. Let dry.

5 Do not wash garment for at least 1 week. Turn garment wrong side out, wash by hand, and hang to dry.

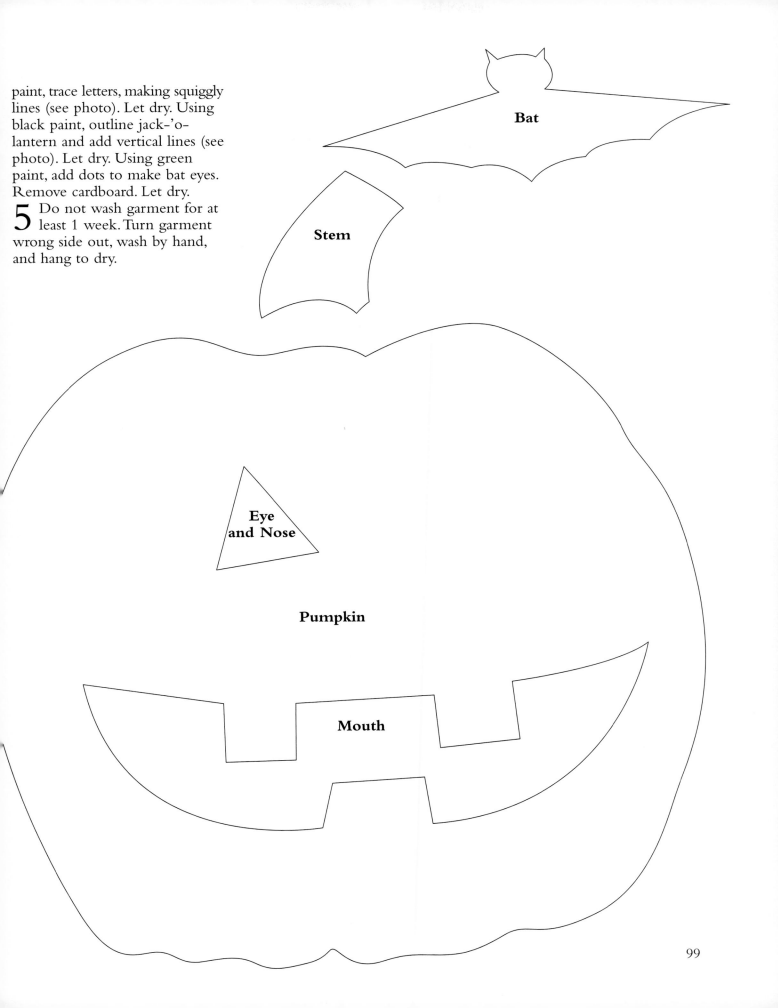

Bat

Stem

Eye and Nose

Pumpkin

Mouth

Pajama Party

Fusible web and holiday fabric create Santa-friendly nightclothes.

Materials

Purchased pajamas or nightshirt
Fabric with holiday designs
Aleene's Original Fusible Web™

Directions

Note: See page 6 for tips on working with fusible web.

Wash and dry garment and fabric; do not use fabric softener in washer or dryer. Iron as needed to remove wrinkles. Fuse web to back of fabric. Do not remove paper backing. Cut out desired designs from fabric. Arrange designs as desired on garment (see photos for inspiration). Remove paper backing and fuse designs to garment. To launder, turn garment inside out or place inside pillowcase before washing. Wash in cold water on gentle cycle. Hang or lay flat to dry.

Designs by Darsee Lett and Pattie Donham

Pins to Please

Turn your favorite fabric motif into a unique pin.

Materials for each pin
Fabrics with desired print
Light cardboard
Aleene's Instant Decoupage™:
 gloss
Aleene's Premium Designer
 Brush™: 12 shader
Dimensional fabric paints to
 match chosen fabric
Aleene's Ultimate Glue Gun™
Aleene's All-purpose Glue Sticks™
Assorted buttons to match fabric
Doily (optional)
Pin back

Directions
Roughly cut out desired design from fabric (see photo). Cut cardboard slightly larger than fabric design. Apply even coat of Instant Decoupage to cardboard, using brush. Lay fabric right side up on cardboard and brush 1 coat of Instant Decoupage over fabric. Let dry. (Instant Decoupage dries clear.) Carefully cut out shape. Using dimensional paints, add details to fabric design. Let dry. Embellish as desired, using buttons and doily (see photo). Let dry. Glue design to pin back. Let dry.

Designs by Cheryl Ball, SCD

Holiday

**Celebrate any occasion
with these festive designs.**

Page 140

Crafting

Ring in the New

Surprise your guests on New Year's Eve with handmade party poppers.

Materials
Aleene's BoxBlanks™
Aleene's Crafting Tissue™ in desired colors
Spray adhesive
Aleene's BoxMaker™
Aleene's Ultimate Glue Gun™
Aleene's All-Purpose Glue Sticks™
Candy or small trinkets to fill popper
Ribbon or cording
Charms, buttons, ribbon roses, or other
    embellishments

Directions

1 **For each,** cut 4½" square from BoxBlank. Cut 4½" x 9" piece from tissue paper. Spray 1 coat of adhesive on 1 side of BoxBlank square. Center tissue on BoxBlank, leaving 2¼" margins at opposite ends. Smooth out wrinkles or bubbles, using fingers. To make fringed edges, cut excess tissue every ¼", from edge of paper to BoxBlank square.

2 Place BoxBlank, with blank side up, onto BoxMaker scoring board and score every 1". (Distance from final scoring to edge of BoxBlank is ½".) Fold box along scored lines. Overlap first section and ½" extension; glue to secure, using glue gun. Let dry.

3 Place candy or trinkets into box and tie ends, using ribbon or cording. Glue charms or other embellishments to box as desired (see photo). Let dry.

Design by Heidi Borchers, SCD

Packaged with Love

Delicately decorated Valentine bags are sure to please your sweetie.

Materials

For each: **Assorted large pink fabric scraps**
Aleene's Fusible Web™
Small white paper bag with handles
Aleene's Thick Designer Tacky Glue™
Adhesive-backed hook-and-loop tape dots
For heart bag: **Dimensional paints: white, pink**
10" length ribbon to coordinate with fabric scraps
White button
For doily bag: **Small Battenberg lace doily**
Dimensional paint: white
½ yard ribbon to coordinate with fabric scraps

Directions

Note: See page 6 for tips on working with fusible web.

1 **For each,** cut 2 (10") squares from 1 fabric. Fuse web to wrong side of 1 fabric square. Remove paper backing and fuse to second fabric square, with wrong sides together. Transfer desired pattern to fused fabric square and cut out.

2 **For heart bag,** transfer heart pattern to paper side of fusible web. Fuse to pink fabric scrap and cut out. Remove paper backing and fuse heart to fabric flap (see photo).

3 **For doily bag,** glue doily to fabric flap (see photo). Let dry.

4 **For each,** cut off handles from 1 side of bag. Position fabric flap on front of bag so that about 1" of flap overlaps onto side of bag with handles (see photo); mark position of remaining handles. Cut 1" slit in flap at each mark, ending with small circular hole (see pattern). Position flap on bag, sliding handles through slits and fitting them into small circular holes. Glue 1" flap overlap to back of bag. Let dry.

5 Fold flap to front of bag. Secure 1 side of hook-and-loop tape dot to wrong side of flap at point. Place remaining side of dot on bag to close as desired. Using dimensional paints, add wavy lines, small hearts, or other details as desired (see photo). Let dry. Tie ribbon in bow and glue in place (see photo). **For heart bag,** glue button to center front of flap (see photo). Let dry.

Enlarge patterns 200%, using photocopier.

Edible "dirt" and "grass"
decorated with Shrink-It™
carrots and bunnies provide a
winsome Easter dessert.

Design by Joan Fee

Hoppy Easter!

Materials for 2 pots
Aleene's Opake Shrink-It™ Plastic
Fine-grade sandpaper
Fine-tip permanent markers:
   black, pink, green, and
   orange; gold (optional)
Aleene's Baking Board™ or non-
   stick cookie sheet, sprinkled
   with baby powder
2 (3½"-diameter) clay pots
Waxed paper
Shortening
Flour
Purchased cake mix
Toothpick
Coconut
Green food coloring
Small bowl
Frosting
Chocolate cookies, finely crushed
Jelly beans

Directions

Note: See page 7 for tips on working with Shrink-It. You need 1 bunny and 1 carrot for each pot.

1 Sand 1 side of each piece of Shrink-It so that markings will adhere. Sand thoroughly both vertically and horizontally. Using black marker, trace patterns (see page 110) onto sanded side of Shrink-It. Cut out patterns.

2 Preheat toaster oven or conventional oven to 275° to 300°. Bake in oven. Let cool. Using permanent markers, color bunny noses and carrots. (For more intense colors, color designs before baking.) Set designs aside.

3 Line clay pots with waxed paper. Spread shortening around inside of pot. Sprinkle small amount of flour into pot; shake to coat and pour out excess. Prepare cake mix, following manufacturer's directions. Pour batter into pots, filling each about halfway. Bake 40 minutes at 350° or until toothpick inserted into center of each cake comes out clean. Let cool. Trim waxed paper even with cake.

4 For "grass," place coconut into bowl, add few drops of green food coloring, and shake coconut in bowl to coat (see photo).

5 Spread frosting over top of each cake. While frosting is still soft, sprinkle with chocolate cookie crumbs for "dirt" or coconut for "grass" as desired; press lightly into frosting (see photo). Press jelly beans into frosting. Press bunny and carrot into frosting and cake to secure. If desired, write greeting or name onto clay pot, using gold marker.

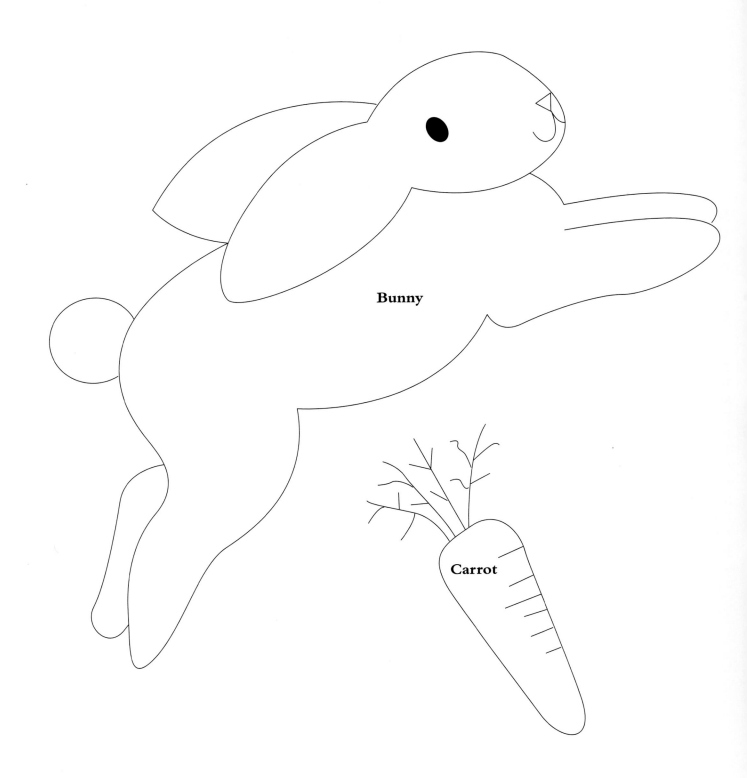

Bunny

Carrot

Liberty Angels

Show your spirit with all-American angels, made from brown bags and craft foam.

Materials
For each: Wooden skewer
Drill with drill bit slightly thicker than skewer
Wooden cutouts: 2½"-wide x ½"-thick star, ¾"-thick 6"-square block
Aleene's Premium-Coat™ Acrylic Paints: Deep Lavender, True Red, White, Gold, Blush
Assorted Aleene's Premium Designer Brushes™
1"-square sponge
Brown bag
Aleene's Tacky Glue™
2" cardboard squeegee
Fun Foam
Pencil
Aleene's Satin Sheen™ Twisted Ribbon: white, red
4" length 28-gauge wire
10" length each embroidery floss: red, white
Embroidery or tapestry needle
Fine-tip permanent black marker

Designs by Heidi Borchers

Directions
Note: Wooden block becomes base for angel.

1 Drill hole through center of wooden star. Drill ½"-deep hole in center of wooden block. Using brush and Deep Lavender, paint top and sides of base. Let dry. Using square sponge, sponge-paint alternating True Red and White squares along edges of base. Let dry. Using brush, paint star Gold. Let dry.

2 From brown bag, cut 4 (9") squares. With edges aligned, glue brown bag squares together, applying 1 coat of glue between layers with squeegee. Let glue dry for few minutes. Transfer patterns to glued bag for 1 body, 1 head, 2 wings, 2 sleeves, 2 hands, and 1 feet; cut out. Transfer heart or large star pattern to brown bag twice and cut out. Shape each piece as desired (see photos). Referring to photo for inspiration, paint background colors and stripes on pieces as desired. Let dry.

3 Cut 1 small star from Fun Foam. Glue 1 side to pencil end of eraser. Let dry. Dip foam star into White and stamp stars on base and body (see photos). **For angel with hearts,** stamp stars on hearts. Let dry. **For angel with stars,** use end of paintbrush to paint dots on brown-bag stars (see photo on page 111). Let dry.

4 **For each,** glue angel pieces together, using photo as guide. Let dry. Cut wooden skewer to desired length; glue to back of angel body. Let dry. Glue small piece of brown bag over skewer on body to secure. Let dry. Place wooden star onto wooden base, matching holes. Place skewer into holes and glue in place. Let dry.

5 For angel's hair, untwist 3" length of white twisted ribbon. **For angel with hearts,** tear twisted ribbon into ⅛"- to ¹⁄₁₆"-wide strips and glue along sides of face; for bangs, glue ¾"-wide strip of fringed twisted ribbon to top of head (see photo). Let dry. **For angel with stars,** cut 1 ribbon piece slightly longer and wider than head and shape (see photo on page 111). Cut top extension at ⅛" intervals. Glue to sides of head. Let dry.

6 **For each,** make halo by shaping wire into circle and twisting ends together. Glue stem to back of head. Let dry. Using embroidery floss and needle, pierce hands and pull length of red floss through (see photos). Glue hearts or stars to ends of floss. Let dry. Tear each color of twisted ribbon into narrow strips. Holding several strips of each color together, tie strips in bow at bottom of angel (see photos). Cut 3" length of white embroidery floss; tie in bow and glue at neck of angel. Let dry. Use black marker to draw facial features.

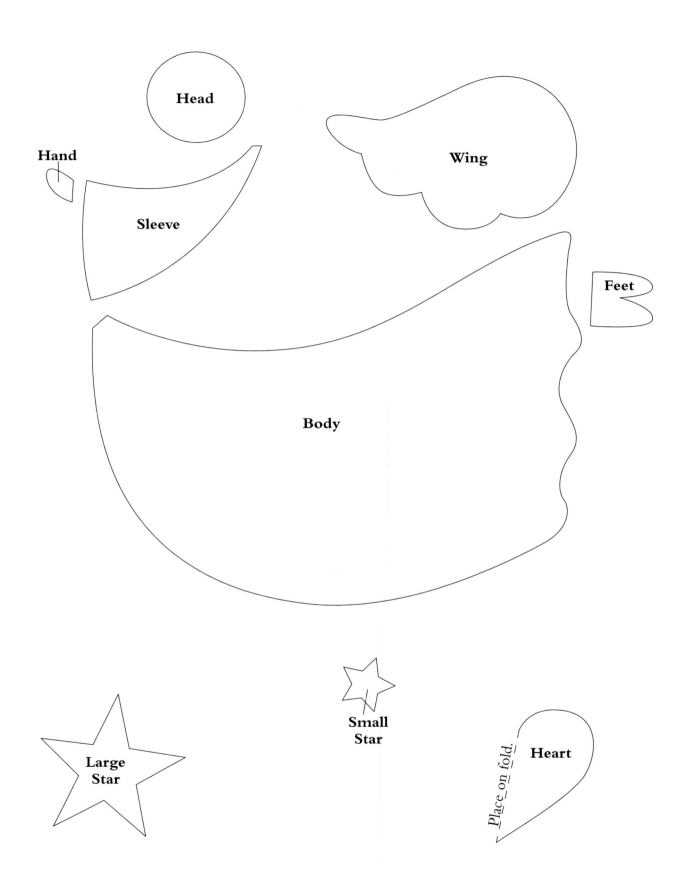

Head

Hand

Wing

Sleeve

Feet

Body

Small
Star

Large
Star

Place on fold.

Heart

★Firecracker ★Cans

Tinsel pipe cleaners top painted cans for a patriotic centerpiece.

Design by Cheryl Ball, SCD

Materials
Aleene's Enhancers™: All-Purpose Primer, Gloss Varnish
Sponge paintbrushes
3 clean, empty tin cans
Aleene's Premium-Coat™ Acrylic Paints: True Red, True Lavender, White, Medium Lavender, Light Blue
Fine-tip permanent black marker
Pop-up craft sponges
Cotton swabs
Aleene's Shrink-It™ Plastic: red
3 each tinsel pipe cleaners: red, blue, silver
Pencil
Ice pick or nail

Directions

1 Apply 1 coat of primer to outside of cans. Let dry. Paint 1 can True Red, 1 can True Lavender, and remaining can White. Let dry. Add second coat if needed and let dry.

2 Using black marker, transfer large, medium, and small star patterns to craft sponges and cut out. Place each sponge into water to expand and wring out excess water. **For red can,** paint stripes with White (see photo). Let dry. Dip large star sponge into True Lavender and sponge-paint star on top of can. Let dry. Add dots to top of can, using cotton swab and White. Let dry. **For lavender can,** dip medium star sponge into White and sponge-paint stars on side and top of can. Let

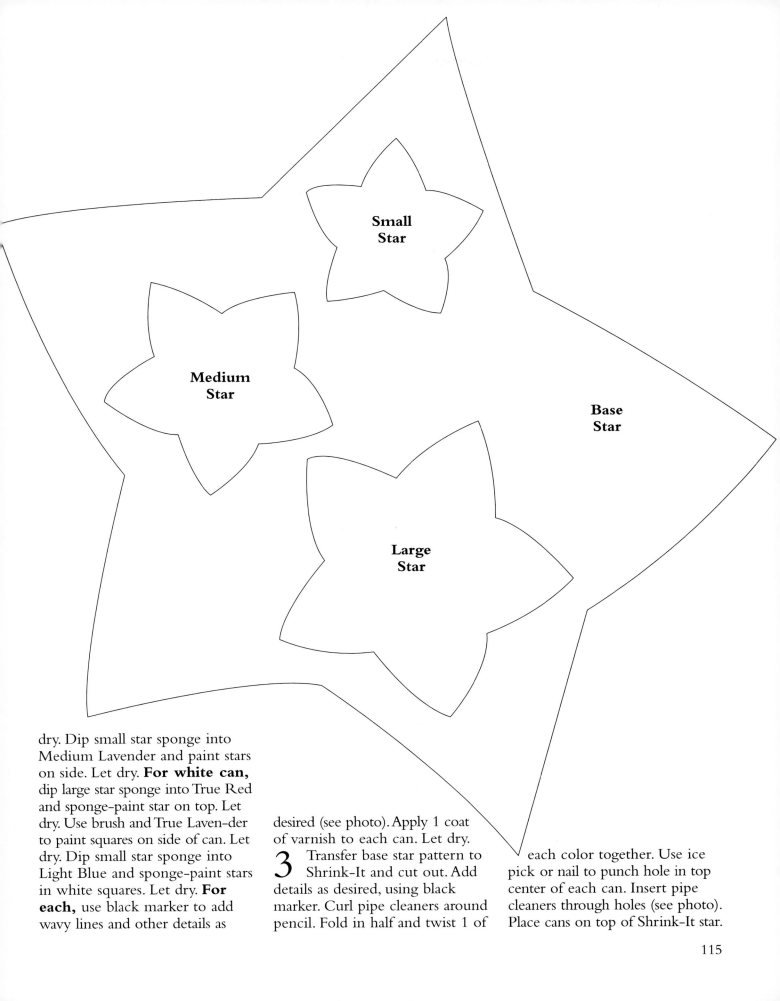

Small Star

Medium Star

Base Star

Large Star

dry. Dip small star sponge into Medium Lavender and paint stars on side. Let dry. **For white can,** dip large star sponge into True Red and sponge-paint star on top. Let dry. Use brush and True Laven-der to paint squares on side of can. Let dry. Dip small star sponge into Light Blue and sponge-paint stars in white squares. Let dry. **For each,** use black marker to add wavy lines and other details as

desired (see photo). Apply 1 coat of varnish to each can. Let dry.

3 Transfer base star pattern to Shrink-It and cut out. Add details as desired, using black marker. Curl pipe cleaners around pencil. Fold in half and twist 1 of

each color together. Use ice pick or nail to punch hole in top center of each can. Insert pipe cleaners through holes (see photo). Place cans on top of Shrink-It star.

115

Witchy Woman

Abracadabra! A plastic soda bottle becomes a candy-holding witch.

Materials
Aleene's Satin Sheen Twisted
 Ribbon™: green, black, orange,
 beige, white
Aleene's Ultimate Glue Gun™
Aleene's All-Purpose Glue Sticks™
Fiberfill
Clean, empty 2-liter soda bottle
2 (1") wiggle eyes
Dimensional paints: black, green
1"-diameter craft foam ball
6" length 18-gauge green florist's
 wire
Pencil
Candy corn

Directions
Note: When working with twisted ribbon, cut specified length and then untwist it, unless directed otherwise.

1 For nose, fold 5" length of green twisted ribbon in half lengthwise. Transfer nose pattern to ribbon and cut out. Glue long edges together. Let dry. Stuff lightly with fiberfill.

2 For hat, cut 2 (10") lengths of black twisted ribbon into triangles of desired length (see photo). Stack pieces, with edges aligned, and glue long edges together to form cone. Let dry. Stuff lightly with fiberfill. For brim, cut 2 (8") lengths of black twisted ribbon. Stack pieces, with edges aligned, and glue together. Let dry. Cut 8"-diameter circle from glued

length; then cut 1½"-diameter circle out of center of first circle. Glue hat to brim, aligning edges of cone with edges of inner circle. Let dry. Cut 12" length of orange twisted ribbon; to not untwist. Cut 1"-wide strip from length and glue around base of hat; trim excess. Tear remaining untwisted orange length into narrow strips. Holding several strips together, tie in bow and glue to hat (see photo). Let dry. Set aside.

3 For hair, shred 2 (18") lengths of beige twisted ribbon into narrow strips. Separate into 2 bundles; tie each bundle in knot at center. Glue 1 bundle to each side of bottle at neck. Let dry. To make bangs, tear 3" length of beige twisted ribbon into narrow strips. Glue strips to bottle below 1 bundle of hair (see photo). Glue on wiggle eyes. Let dry. Glue nose in place. Let dry.

4 For clothes, transfer sleeve pattern to 6" length of black twisted ribbon twice and cut out. Transfer hand pattern to 2" length of white twisted ribbon twice and cut out. Glue 1 hand to each sleeve. Let dry. Glue 1 sleeve to each side of bottle (see photo). Let dry. Using black dimensional paint, draw wart on nose and smile on bottle (see photo). Let dry.

5 For pumpkin, cut 5" length of orange twisted ribbon. Wrap around foam craft ball to

cover; secure with glue. Trim any excess. Let dry. Cut ¼" length of green twisted ribbon; do not untwist. Glue to top of pumpkin for stem. Let dry. Using black dimensional paint, draw face on pumpkin (see photo). Let dry. Glue pumpkin to hands (see photo). Let dry.

6 For bat, transfer pattern to leftover untwisted black twisted ribbon and cut out. Using green dimensional paint, draw eyes on bat (see photo). Let dry. Curl wire around pencil. Glue 1 end of coil to back of bat. Let dry. Insert free end of coil into top of pumpkin. Fill bottle with candy corn. Place hat on top of bottle.

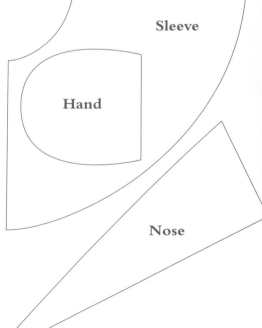

Sleeve

Hand

Nose

Bat

Design by Joan Fee, SCD

Pumpkin Mobile

Connect Shrink-It™ jack-o'-lanterns to make a mobile or use them individually to adorn cupcakes and other party items.

Materials
4 sheets Aleene's Clear Shrink-It™ Plastic
Black dimensional paint
Aleene's Crafting Tissue Paper: orange, brown, green
Aleene's Reverse Collage Glue™
½"-wide shader paintbrush
Hole punch
Monofilament thread
Suction cups with hangers

Directions

1 Trace patterns onto Shrink-It desired number of times, using dimensional paint and leaving about ¾" between designs. Let dry. Place Shrink-It facedown. Using orange for pumpkin, brown for stems, and green for leaves, place tissue paper over back of Shrink-It and trace designs. Cut out tissue paper ¼" outside traced lines. For each, crumple each tissue-paper piece and then flatten, leaving some wrinkles. Working over 1 design area at a time, brush 1 coat of Reverse Collage Glue onto Shrink-It where desired. Press corresponding tissue-paper piece into glue-covered area. Working from outside edges to center, use fingers or brush to shape piece to fit design area (see photo). Brush 1 coat of glue on top of tissue paper. In same manner, glue remaining tissue-paper pieces in place on design.

2 Retrace pattern lines on tissue-paper side of Shrink-It, using dimensional paint. Let dry. Cut out, following outside edge of design. Using hole punch, make small hole in stem (see photo).

3 String pumpkins together as desired, using monofilament thread. Tie mobile to suction cups and hang from window or mirror.

Design by Darsee Lett and Pattie Donham

Turkey Time

Welcome holiday family and friends with a colorful turkey in your yard.

Materials

1 fence post
3 vinyl place mats
Sanding sponge
Tack cloth
Aleene's Essentials: Burnt Umber
Aleene's Premium-Coat™ Acrylic
    Paints: Deep Sage, True Poppy,
    True Orange, True Apricot,
    Ivory, True Red
1" flat paintbrush
Pop-up craft sponges
Waxed paper
Paper towels
Fine-tip permanent black marker
Cotton swabs
Aleene's OK to Wash-It Glue™
¾" brass nails
Hammer
Aleene's Enhancers™: Gloss Varnish
Raffia
Silk flower with leaves

Directions

1 Sand fence post and back of place mats to roughen surfaces for painting. Wipe with tack cloth to remove dust. Paint top half of fence post Burnt Umber and bottom half Deep Sage. Paint back of 2 place mats True Poppy. Paint half of back of remaining place mat True Poppy and other half True Orange. Let dry.

2 Transfer tail pattern (1) to True Poppy place mats 7 times; cut out. Transfer wattle pattern (2) to True Poppy section of remaining place mat and cut out. Transfer beak pattern (3) to True Orange section of remaining place mat and cut out.

3 Transfer large crescent (4), small crescent (5), and triangle (6) patterns to pop-up sponges and cut out. Place each sponge into water to expand and wring out excess water. Pour puddle of True Apricot onto waxed paper. Dip large crescent-shaped sponge into paint and blot excess on paper towel. Press onto curved ends of tail sections, reloading with paint as necessary. Let dry. Using black marker, draw line from below crescent shape to end of each tail section (see photo).

4 Lay tail sections on work surface so that curved ends of 3 face left and curved ends of remaining sections face right. Dip wedge-shaped sponge into True Orange and press above drawn lines, reloading with paint as necessary. Repeat to paint Deep Sage triangles below lines (see photo). Let dry. Using cotton swabs and Ivory, paint dot at 1 end of each line, just below large crescent shape (see photo). Let dry.

5 Using small crescent-shaped sponge and Ivory, paint

shapes on fence post (see photo). Let dry. Paint beak True Apricot and wattle True Red. Let dry. Glue beak and wattle to fence post (see photo). Let dry. Using black marker, draw eyes; highlight eyes with cotton swab and Ivory. Let dry.

6 Working from back of post, center 1 tail section above head, allowing curved end to extend about 3" (see photo). Glue in place. Let dry. Secure with nails. With Deep Sage triangles at bottom, position remaining tail sections 1 at a time, referring to photo for placement; glue and nail each in place. Let dry.

7 For sign, cut 4½" x 10½" rectangle from remaining True Orange place-mat section, scalloping edges (see photo). Using black marker, write "Give Thanks," adding dots and lines as desired (see photo). Glue and then nail sign at slight angle below turkey. Nail through ends of letters and color nailheads with black marker.

8 Apply 1 coat of varnish to entire project. Let dry. Tie raffia bow around turkey's neck. Insert flower behind sign and glue in place. Let dry.

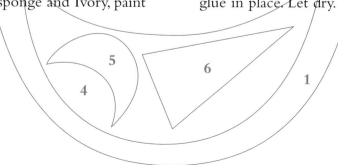

Design by Cheryl Ball, SCD

3-D Tree

Deck your halls with a three-dimensional Shrink-It™ Christmas tree.

Materials
Aleene's Opake Shrink-It™ Plastic
Fine-grade sandpaper
Fine-tip permanent black marker
Colored pencils, fabric markers, or acrylic paints in desired colors
Fabric glitter paints: green, gold
½" flat paintbrush
Hole punch
Aleene's Baking Board™ or non-stick cookie sheet, sprinkled with baby powder
Craft rhinestones in assorted colors
Ornament hanger
Aleene's Jewel-It Glue™

Directions

Note: See page 7 for tips on working with Shrink-It.

1 Sand both sides of Shrink-It so that markings will adhere. Be sure to sand thoroughly both vertically and horizontally. Using black marker, transfer patterns to 1 side of Shrink-It. Then turn Shrink-It over and trace pattern markings onto opposite side.

2 Color trees and stars on both sides as desired, using colored pencils, fabric markers, or acrylic paints. Let dry, if necessary. (Colored pencils create pastel finish. Fabric markers retain color vibrancy after shrinking. For acrylic paints, thin with water first to prevent cracking when plastic shrinks; acrylic paints produce dull matte finish after shrinking.

3 Thin glitter paints with water to milky consistency. Using paintbrush, lightly apply green glitter paint to desired areas of trees and gold glitter paint to stars (see photo). Let dry. (Glitter paint may appear sparse, but shrinking will concentrate it.)

4 Preheat toaster oven or conventional oven to 275° to 300°. Cut out painted designs. Using hole punch, make hole in top of star with rounded top for hanger. Bake designs in oven. Let cool.

5 Assemble ornament by sliding pieces together and glue to secure. Let dry. Glue on rhinestones as desired for ornaments (see photo). Let dry. Insert ornament hanger through hole in star.

Design by Joann Pearson

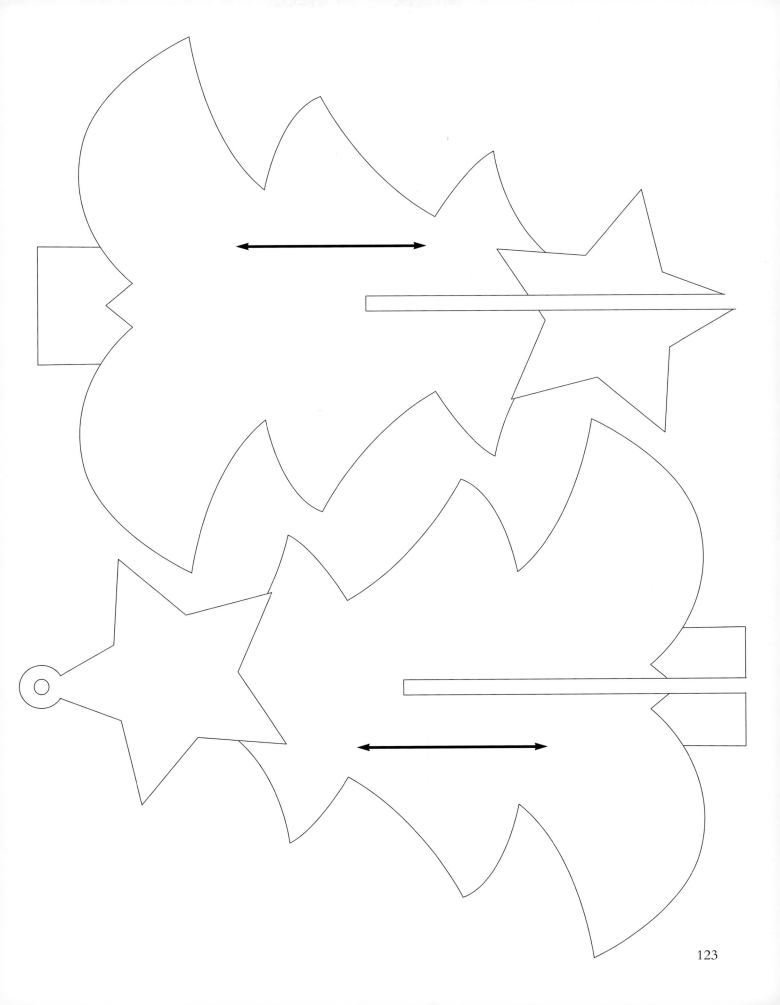

123

Wired Star

Flexible craft wire is so easy to work with, you can fashion a star in a twinkling.

Materials
Wood scrap (larger than star design)
Hammer
10 nails
20-gauge craft wire: silver, gold
Wire cutters
Needle-nosed pliers
Monofilament thread

Directions

Transfer star pattern to wood. Hammer 1 nail into each star point and into each inner corner of design, leaving ½" of nail exposed. Wind silver wire around nails (see photos), using pliers to create sharp corners. Outline star 4 times with silver wire; then cut wire. To secure ends of wire, tuck between other wires. Remove star from board. To finish, treat silver wires as 1 unit and wrap gold wire around star, forming loose spirals and loops (see photos). Cut excess wire and secure ends by tucking between other wires. Cut 9" length of monofilament thread, loop through top of star, and knot to form hanger.

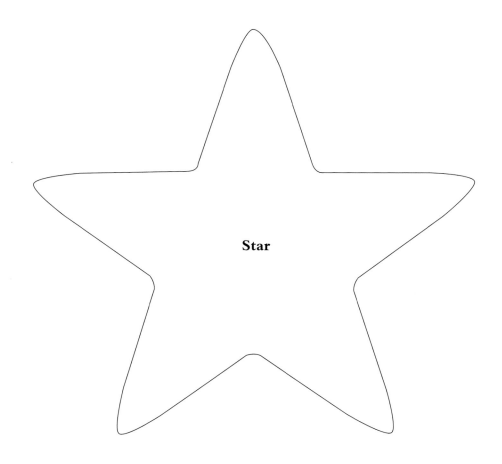

Star

Hammer nails into star points and corners.

Wind silver wire around nails.

Remove star from board and wrap gold wire around star.

125

Homespun Holidays

Ho, ho, ho! This tree skirt is no sew.

Materials
36"-diameter natural canvas tree skirt
Fabrics: 12" x 18" rectangle green plaid, 11" square burgundy plaid, brown scraps
17" square fusible web
Disappearing-ink fabric marker
Delta Ceramcoat® Gleems: 14 karat gold
Delta Ceramcoat® Acrylic Paints: Sweetheart Blush, Hunter Green
Small flat paintbrush
2 (1"-wide) wooden stars
Aleene's Tacky Glue™
Gold buttons: 24 small, 2 large
Cording: 60" metallic gold-red-and-green twisted without lip, 1¼ yards metallic gold, 3 yards plus 8" (⅜"-wide) metallic gold-red-and-green twisted with lip
7 (3"-long) metallic gold-red-and-green tassels
7 jingle bells
3 yards plus 8" (1"-wide) metallic gold-red-and-green looped fringe
3M Scotch™Guard Spray (optional)

Directions
Note: See page 6 for tips on working with fusible web.

1 Wash and dry tree skirt and fabrics; do not use fabric softener in washer or dryer. Iron as needed to remove wrinkles.

2 Transfer patterns (see page 128) to fusible web and cut 2 hearts, 2 trees, and 4 squares ⅛" outside marked lines. Fuse web designs to wrong side of fabric pieces as follows: trees and 2 square patches to green plaid, hearts to burgundy plaid, and remaining squares to brown scraps.

3 Fuse 1 tree and 1 brown square to tree skirt, positioning trunk about 2" from bottom edge of skirt and slightly overlapping tree on trunk (see photo). Position another tree and trunk on opposite side of tree skirt and fuse in place. Center hearts between trees, placing points about 2" from bottom edge of skirt. Fuse in place. Fuse 1 green plaid square to 1 side of heart (see photo).

4 Complete 1 pair of mittens at a time. Using disappearing-ink marker, transfer mitten pattern (see page 128) and reversed mitten pattern (including snowflake design) to tree skirt between 1 heart and tree (see photo). Paint snowflake in center of each mitten, using paintbrush and 14 karat gold paint. Let dry. Paint triangles, using Sweetheart Blush. Let dry. Using Hunter Green, paint mitten outline in 1 brush stroke; then paint dashes. Let dry. Repeat to mark and paint pairs of mittens between each heart and tree.

5 Paint wooden stars, using 14 karat gold paint. Let dry. Glue 1 star to top of each tree (see photo). Let dry. Glue 12 small gold buttons to each tree for ornaments. Let dry. Glue 1 large button to each heart patch. Let dry. Cut 4 (15") lengths of twisted cording without lip, allowing ends to ravel slightly. Referring to photo, glue cording ends to mittens, looping cording above mittens. Glue loop to secure. Let dry.

6 Cut 7 (6") lengths of gold cording and tie 1 around binding of each tassel. Tie 1 bell to each end of cording. Slide tassels onto twisted cording with lip. Fold under and glue each end of twisted cording with lip for finished ends. Let dry. Place 1 finished end at tree skirt opening and position around edge of tree skirt, gluing to secure. Adjust tassels as you work so that 1 tassel falls directly below center of each design (see photo), except at opening. Let dry.

7 Fold under 1 end of looped fringe and glue to prevent fraying. Let dry. Glue looped fringe to lip of twisted cording on skirt. Let dry. If desired, spray with ScotchGuard to waterproof and to protect. Let dry.

Design by Lisa Tempesta

127

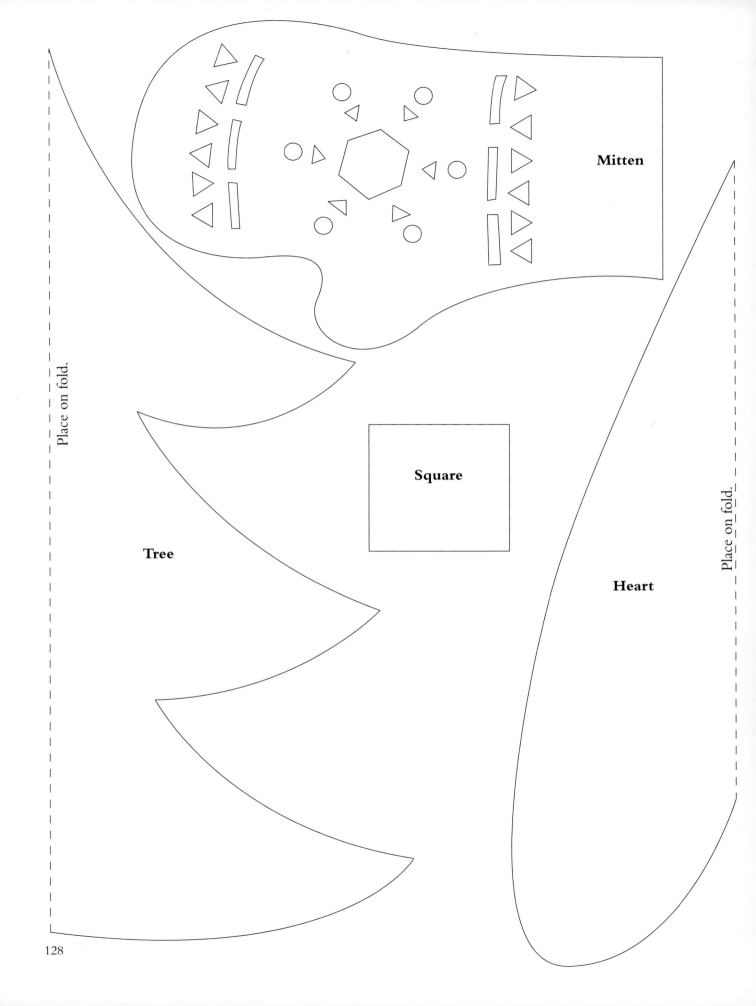

Place on fold.

Mitten

Square

Tree

Heart

Place on fold.

128

Sock It To Me

Feel Christmas cheer right down to your toes when you fuse holiday motifs to your socks.

Designs by Joan Fee

Materials for each pair
Aleene's Fusible Web™
Christmas fabric scrap
Purchased socks in desired color
Gift-wrap tube or small jar
Glitter fabric paint

Directions
Note: See page 6 for tips on working with fusible web.

Fuse web to wrong side of Christmas fabric scrap. Cut out desired motifs. Place 1 sock over gift-wrap tube or jar to stretch sock slightly. Fuse motifs to sock as desired. Using glitter paint, embellish sock as desired (see photos for inspiration). Repeat for remaining sock.

Snazzy Snowman

**Tissue-paper appliqués make
this holiday sweatshirt and gift box
inexpensive as well as
simple to make.**

Materials

For each: Aleene's Crafting Tissue Paper™: black,
   orange, red, green
½"-wide flat paintbrush
For sweatshirt: Purchased white sweatshirt
Cardboard covered with waxed paper
Disappearing-ink pen
Aleene's Paper Napkin Appliqué Glue™
For box: 2 sheets white posterboard
Plates: 1 (6"), 1 (8½"), 1(10")
Pencil
Aleene's Thick Designer Tacky Glue™

Directions for sweatshirt

1 Wash and dry sweatshirt; do not use fabric
   softener in washer or dryer. Iron as needed to
remove wrinkles. Place cardboard covered with
waxed paper inside shirt.

2 For eyes and smile, cut 6 (1") squares from
   black tissue paper. Referring to page 132,
transfer nose pattern to orange tissue paper and
hat pattern to red tissue paper; cut out. From
green tissue paper, cut 1"-diameter circle.

3 Position tissue-paper pieces on sweatshirt to
   form design (see photo). Using disappearing-
ink pen, trace pieces. Removing 1 piece of tissue
at a time, brush glue inside drawn lines. Replace
corresponding tissue-paper piece, pressing into
glue-covered area. Brush another coat of glue on
top of tissue paper, brushing slightly beyond tissue
edges. Let dry.

4 Do not wash for at least 1 week. Turn inside
   out, wash by hand, and hang to dry.

Designs by Joan Fee

131

Directions for box

1 From 1 long edge of each sheet of posterboard, cut 1 (2"-wide) and 1 (2½"-wide) strips (total of 4 strips); set aside. For snowman shape, place plates on posterboard, overlapping edges slightly, and trace around plates, using pencil (see photo). Cut out. Use cutout as pattern to cut 1 more snowman shape from remaining piece of posterboard.

2 On photocopier, reduce hat and nose patterns 87%. For eyes, smile, and buttons, cut 10 (¾") squares from black tissue paper. Transfer nose pattern to orange tissue paper and cut out.

Transfer hat pattern to red tissue paper and to posterboard; cut out. Glue tissue-paper hat to posterboard hat. Let dry. From green tissue paper and posterboard, cut 1½"-diameter circle. Glue tissue-paper circle to posterboard circle. Let dry. Glue green posterboard circle to top of hat (see photo). Let dry.

3 Using 2 black squares for eyes, 3 squares for buttons, and remaining squares for smile, position all tissue-paper pieces and hat on 1 posterboard snowman shape (see photo). Removing 1 piece of tissue at a time, brush glue onto posterboard where tissue will be

placed. Replace corresponding tissue-paper piece, pressing into glue-covered area. Brush another coat of glue on top of tissue paper, brushing slightly beyond tissue edges. Let dry.

4 Glue 2"-wide posterboard strips together, overlapping ends slightly. Let dry. For box bottom, apply bead of glue ¼" from edge of plain snowman shape. Place posterboard strip into glue, bending into snowman shape as you go. Let dry. For box top, follow same procedure, using 2½"-wide strips and gluing close to edge of back of decorated snowman shape. Let dry.

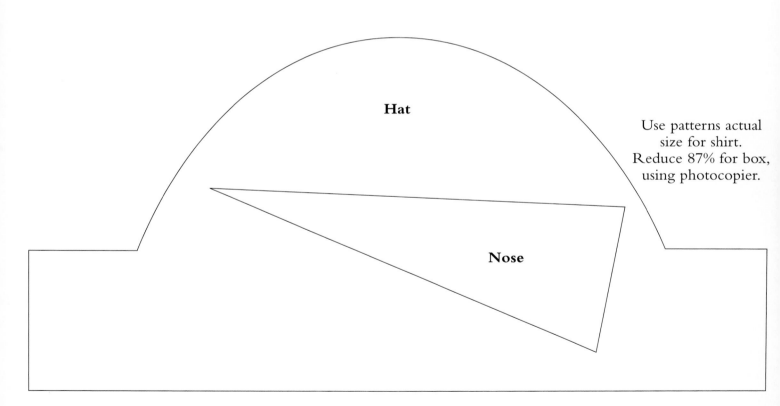

Hat

Nose

Use patterns actual size for shirt. Reduce 87% for box, using photocopier.

Design by Cheryl Ball, SCD

Twinkling Tannenbaum

May your Christmas be merry and bright with a table ornament made from painted boxes and lights.

Materials

4 papier-mâché nesting boxes, ranging in diameter from 5" to 9½"
Aleene's Premium-Coat™ Acrylic Paints: Medium Green, True Green, Holiday Green, Deep Green, Ivory, True Yellow, True Red, True Lavender
Paintbrushes: ½", 1"
Sea sponge
Cotton swabs
Wooden stars: 12 (1"), 1 (3")
20 (½") wooden buttons
Aleene's Enhancers™: Gloss Varnish
Ice pick
4 sets battery-operated white Christmas minilights
Batteries
Masking tape
Aleene's Thick Designer Tacky Glue™
Toothpick
1 yard 1"-wide ribbon

Directions

1 Starting with smallest box and ending with largest box, paint boxes as follows: Medium Green, True Green, Holiday Green, and Deep Green. Sponge-paint each lid, using mixture of corresponding box color and Ivory. Let dry.

2 Paint details on boxes as follows: **For Medium Green box,** thin Ivory with water; dip cotton swab into thinned paint and dot randomly on box (see photo). Let dry. **For True Green box,** thin Medium Green with water; paint checkerboard design, using brush width of desired checks. Add thin line of Holiday Green on left side of each check (see photo). Let dry. **For Holiday Green box,** thin True Green with water and paint wavy lines; using tip of brush, paint 2 thin strips (see photo). Let dry. **For Deep Green box,** thin Holiday Green with water; paint stripes on box, using 1" brush. Use tip of brush to paint thin stripes on each side of larger stripes (see photo). Let dry.

3 For each, paint 1" stars True Yellow. Let dry. Paint buttons Ivory, True Red, and True Lavender. Let dry. Apply 1 coat of varnish to all pieces. Let dry.

4 Paint checkerboard pattern on 3" star, using True Yellow and Ivory. Paint edges True Lavender. Let dry. Glue button to center front of star. Let dry.

5 Using ice pick, punch 1 hole in side of 1 box for each light on strand. Place lights inside box and push bulbs through holes. Use masking tape to secure lights inside box. Repeat for remaining boxes.

6 Glue buttons and stars to boxes as desired (see photo). Let dry. Glue toothpick to back of 3" star. Let dry. Tie ribbon in multilooped bow; notch ends and glue to back of star (see photo). Let dry. Poke small hole in lid of smallest box and insert free end of toothpick. Referring to photo, glue bottom of Holiday Green box to Deep Green lid, bottom of True Green box to Holiday Green lid, and bottom of Medium Green box to True Green lid. Let dry. Place batteries in lights and put lids on boxes.

Golden Angels

Add a divine touch to your tree with these engaging angels.

Design by Heidi Borchers

Materials

For each: Aleene's BoxBlanks™
Aleene's Premium-Coat™ Acrylic
    Paint: Blush
Aleene's Premium Designer
    Brush™: #12 shader
Hole punches: ¼", ⅛"
Aleene's Decoupage Paper:
    Poppies and Tulips
Aleene's Tacky Glue™
Fine-tip permanent black marker
Copper kitchen metal scrubber
2 (½") star sequins
Gold spray paint
Aleene's Instant Decoupage™:
    matte
Aleene's 3D Foiling Glue™
Aleene's Crafting Foil™: gold
12" length gold wire
Pencil
Aleene's Satin Sheen Twisted
    Ribbon™: beige
4" length ⅛"-wide ribbon
    (optional)

Directions

Note: Use Tacky Glue unless otherwise specified.

1 Transfer body/wings and head patterns to BoxBlank. Then draw ½" x 1½" rectangle. Cut out patterns and rectangle.

2 Paint head Blush. Let dry. Using ¼" hole punch, cut 2 circles from edge of pink area of decoupage paper. Glue circles to face for cheeks (see photo). Let dry. Using black marker, draw facial features. Glue face to rectangle so that rectangle extends ½" below bottom of face. Let dry. Cut and glue small section of copper scrubber to head for hair (see photo). Glue 1 star sequin to hair as desired. Let dry.

3 Spray-paint body/wings gold. Let dry. Transfer body pattern to decoupage paper and cut out. Apply 1 coat of Instant Decoupage to angel body. Position paper cutout on body. Smooth out wrinkles and bubbles, using fingers. Brush another coat of Instant Decoupage over paper. Let dry.

4 Apply 3-D Foiling Glue as desired to angel (see photo for inspiration). Let dry. (Glue will be opaque and sticky when dry.) To apply foil, lay foil dull side down on top of glue lines. Using fingers, gently but firmly press foil into glue, completeley covering glue. Peel away foil paper.

5 Using Tacky Glue, glue rectangle extension of head to back of body. Let dry. For hanger, punch ⅛" holes on both sides of wings (see photo). Curl wire around pencil. Working from front to back, insert 1 end of wire through each hole. Twist to secure.

6 Untwist 24" length of twisted ribbon. Tear into narrow strips. Holding several strips together, tie strips in bow around hanger. Glue remaining star sequin to center of bow. Let dry. If desired, tie ribbon in bow and glue to neck. Let dry.

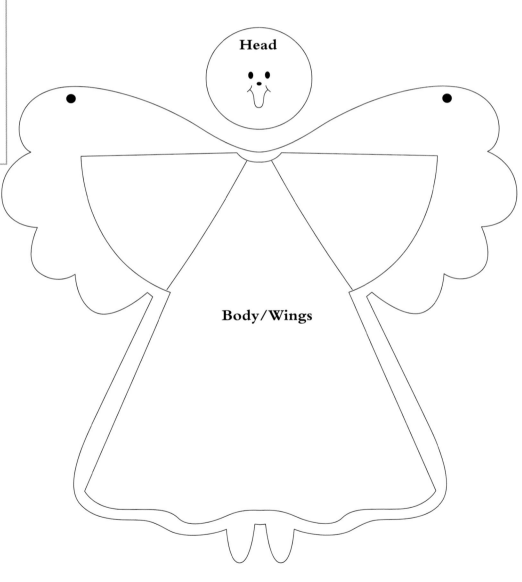

Head

Body/Wings

Star Shine

Turning a recycled yogurt lid into an ornament makes a happier holiday for you *and* for the environment.

Materials

Clean, dry yogurt lid with clear insert
Rubbing alcohol (optional)
Cotton swab (optional)
Tulip® 3D Paints™: Slick Black, Glitter Gold, Slick Dusty Rose, Pearl Snow White, Pearl Violet, Glitter Silver
Tulip® & Scribbles™ 3D Paint™ Design Tools: TL490 TIPS, TL 496 Design Tool (optional)
Decorative string, ribbon, or other trim for hanger
Aleene's Thick Designer Tacky Glue™ (optional)
Hole punch (optional)
Tulip® & Scribbles™ 3D Paint™ Sealers: Gloss Sealer
½" flat, soft paintbrush

Directions

1 Remove any product dating and numbers on top of lid, using small amount of alcohol on cotton swab. (Do not use fingernail polish remover or acetone because these products will cloud clear surface.) Center clear lid over pattern; with black 3D paint, outline star. (If desired, use fine-line tip on paint bottle.) Referring to photo, outline sections in various mosaic shapes. Run ring of black paint around inner edge of lid. Lay flat to let dry 5 to 10 minutes.

2 Fill in star with Glitter Gold paint, working from center of star toward edges of lid. Fill in sections in desired colors, touching tip of paint bottle to open area and moving tip back and forth within area to fill. Lay flat and let dry 30 to 45 minutes.

3 Cut string, ribbon, or trim to make hanger. Glue in place; or punch hole in top center of ornament, put string, ribbon, or trim through, and tie to secure. Let glue dry.

4 When complete, let ornament dry at least 72 hours. Then apply 1 coat of 3D Gloss Sealer on top of painted surface, using flat brush. Let dry.

Star

Use rubbing alcohol to clean any writing from a clear yogurt lid.

Design by Lee Riggins-Hartman

Heaven Scent Angel

This angel has a mission: she covers a room air freshener.

Materials

2 (2"-diameter) craft foam balls
Serrated knife
Aleene's Ultimate Glue Gun™
Aleene's All-Purpose Glue Sticks™
Adjustable, refillable room air freshener
¼ yard muslin
Rotary cutter with scallop blade, cutting mat, and acrylic ruler; or pinking shears
Sewing machine (optional)
Thread to match muslin
Hand-sewing needle
Aleene's Premium-Coat™ Acrylic Paints: Soft Beige, Black
Paintbrushes: #12 shader, ½" flat, ¼" short-bristle
6" beige chenille stem, cut in half
4" square beige felt
Curly raffia hair: 2 (20") lengths, scraps
2 straight pins with large black plastic heads
Tracing paper
5½" x 8½" piece posterboard
Wooden shapes: 120 medium teardrops, 2 large stars, 4 medium stars, 5 small stars
Aleene's Tacky Glue™
36" length 24-gauge gold or brass wire
Pliers or wire cutters
Rub-on gold leaf finisher (optional)
24" length ½"-wide gold mesh ribbon

Design by Cindy Groom-Harry® and Staff

Directions

1 For torso, cut 1"-diameter slice off bottom and top of 1 foam ball, using knife. Glue 1 flat side of ball to top of air freshener cover, using glue gun. Let dry.

2 For dress, cut 8½" x 22" piece from muslin. Trim ¼" on 1 long side for hem, using rotary cutter with scallop blade or pinking shears. With right sides together, glue or machine-stitch short sides together. Make ½"-long basting stitches ¼" below top straight edge of dress. Pull thread ends to gather dress to form tight circle. Knot thread ends and trim excess thread. Slip dress onto foam ball and adjust gathers (see photo). Randomly glue dress to top of shaped foam ball. Let dry.

3 For head, cut 1"-diameter slice off bottom of remaining foam ball. Paint ball with 2 coats of Soft Beige, letting dry after each coat. Glue flat bottom of head to top of dress. Let dry.

4 For each sleeve, cut 4" x 6" piece from remaining muslin. Trim ¼" from 1 long edge for hem, using rotary cutter with scallop blade or pinking shears. Turn 1 short edge under ¼" and glue in place. Let dry. Lap finished short edge of fabric over opposite short edge to form cylinder; glue in place. Let dry. Make ¼" basting stitches around top unfinished edge of sleeve; pull snugly to gather and knot thread ends. Glue sleeve to air freshener cover ⅜" below neck. Let dry. Insert 3" length of chenille stem into sleeve; glue in place. Let dry.

5 For hands, transfer pattern to beige felt twice and cut out. Glue 1 hand to each chenille stem inside sleeve, with stem ending at wrist and thumb pointing toward body. Let dry.

6 For hair, cut 1 length of raffia hair lengthwise into 3 pieces. Stack and bind in center, using raffia scrap. Glue to center top of head. Let dry. Repeat to make second hair section and glue to head directly behind first section. Let dry. Pull hair strands apart, using fingers. When satisfied with arrangement, apply glue to head and press hair into glue. Tear additional raffia into 2" lengths. Roll in hands to make loose ball and arrange on top of head to cover knots and to make bangs. Glue in place. Let dry. For eyes, insert straight pins ¾" apart about halfway down face (see photo).

7 For wings, transfer pattern to folded tracing paper and cut out. Unfold tracing paper, transfer pattern to posterboard and cut out. Referring to photo, attach medium wooden teardrops to 1 side of posterboard wings with Tacky Glue, starting in center of wings and working toward ends. Let dry.

8 For garland, cut 18" length from wire, using pliers or wire cutters. Apply dot of glue to center of 1 large star. Place center of wire into glue; top with second large star, aligning edges and sandwiching wire in between. In same manner, glue 1 pair of medium stars 2" on each side of large stars (see photo). Let dry. If desired, lightly apply gold leaf to edges of stars; then brush gold from edge and blend toward center. Scrunch and bend wire as desired, curling ends. Glue garland to underside of hands and then drape as desired. Let dry.

9 For halo, cut 18" length from wire, using pliers or wire cutters. Coil center of wire into 1½"-diameter circle, wrapping cut ends to secure. Glue 5 small stars side by side on halo (see photo). Let dry. If desired, apply gold leaf to edges of stars. Glue halo to top of head. Let dry.

10 Tie mesh ribbon in bow. Shape tails into spirals and cut ends on diagonal. Glue bow under chin. Let dry.

11 To replace depleted air freshener gel, remove cover with angel attached and discard dried gel. Take nontoxic gel from new container and slip over post of decorated base. Put angel cover back on.

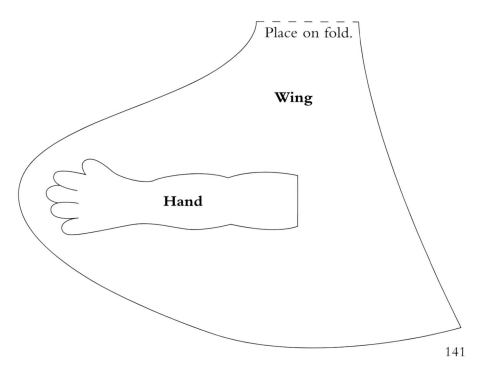

Place on fold.

Wing

Hand

Design by Vickie Walls and
Jan Blackwell for Michaels

Special Delivery

Even your mailbox can be festive for the holidays.

Materials

For each: **PVC Pine Mailbox Cover**
Florist's wire
Wire cutters
Aleene's Ultimate Glue Gun™
Aleene's All-Purpose Glue Sticks™
Standard-sized mailbox
For bird cover: **Ribbons: 2½"-wide red gingham metallic wire-edged, 1½"-wide gold wire-edged**
4 (32") berry sprays
Red bird pick
5 wrapped-package picks
For poinsettia cover: **3 yards sheer snowflake ribbon**
Snow-tipped artificial flower and greenery: red poinsettia bush, holly spray with berries
2 snowman picks
Snowflake garland

Directions

1 **For each,** fluff branches of mailbox cover.

2 **For bird cover,** make multi-looped bow from each ribbon, leaving 30" streamer on left and 18" streamer on right. Notch streamer ends. Place gold bow in center of red gingham bow. Wire in place on arrangement, using florist's wire (see photo at left). Loosely wind berry sprays throughout arrangement and secure with florist's wire. Glue bird pick in place (see photo at left). Let dry. Glue wrapped-package picks to arrangement as desired. Let dry.

3 **For poinsettia cover,** from snowflake ribbon, tie bow as in Step 2. Attach bow to right side of arrangement, using florist's wire (see photo above). Let streamers cascade throughout branches. Cut desired sections of poinsettia bush and glue along arrangement. Let dry. Glue snowman picks to upper left of arrangement; glue holly spray in front of snowmen. Let dry. Cut desired number of snowflakes from garland; glue to tips of branches throughout arrangement. Let dry.

4 **For each,** slide cover over mailbox.

Index